As long as the earth endures,
Seedtime and harvest,
Cold and heat,
Summer and winter,
Day and night
  will never cease.

(*Genesis* 8:22, *New International Version*)

WHILE THE EARTH ENDURES

*A Report on
the Theological and Ethical considerations
of Responsible Land-Use in Scotland*

by

*Members of a Working Party for
the Society, Religion and Technology Project*

SRT PROJECT 1986

Distributed by Quorum Press

EDINBURGH

First published by the SRT Project, 1986
Church of Scotland Department of Ministry and Mission,
and distributed by
The Saint Andrew Press, 121 George Street,
Edinburgh EH2 4YN under the imprint Quorum Press.

ISBN 0 86153 085 3

British Library Cataloguing in Publication Data

While the earth endures: a report on responsible land-use in Scotland.
  1. Land-use – Scotland
  I. Working Party for the Society, Religion and Technology Project
333.73'13'09411 HD616

Typeset, printed and bound by
W. M. Bett Limited, Tillicoultry, Scotland

CONTENTS

Members of Working Party

Mr Roland Bean; Chartered Town Planner, Perth and Kinross District

Dr J. Morton Boyd; Ecological Consultant, former Director NCC

Professor J. B. Caird and Mr Frank Spaven; Scottish Interests Sub-Committee of the Church and Nation Committee

Dr A. J. Crosbie; Head of Department of Geography, University of Edinburgh

Dr Howard H. Davis; former Director, SRT Project

Professor Charles H. Gimingham; Department of Plant Science, University of Aberdeen

Mr John Goodfellow; National Farmers Union of Scotland

Mr Willie Hall; Chairman, Scottish Association of Young Farmers Groups

Dr Ulrich Loening; Reader in the Department of Zoology and Director of the Centre for Human Ecology, University of Edinburgh

Ms Mairi MacArthur; Friends of the Earth (Scotland)

Mrs Abigail Marland; Centre for Human Ecology, University of Edinburgh

Mr Ian Melrose; National Farmers Union of Scotland

Mr Ian Nicholson; formerly Institute of Terrestrial Ecology, Aberdeen; now retired. Contributed in personal capacity

Rev Dr Ruth Page; Lecturer, Department of Systematic Theology, New College, Edinburgh

Mr Charles Somerville; SRT Project, Working Party Convener

David Pullinger, Director, SRT Project (January 1986)

List of Common Abbreviations

CAP	Common Agricultural Policy
CCS	Countryside Commission for Scotland
DAFS	Department of Agriculture and Fisheries, Scotland
EEC	European Economic Community
FFWAG	Farming, Forestry and Wild Life Groups
FOE	Friends of the Earth
Ha	Hectare (1 hectare = 2.47 acres)
ITE	Institute of Terrestrial Ecology
NCC	National Conservancy Council
NFU	National Farmers' Union
NNR	National Nature Reserves
NTS	National Trust for Scotland
RSPB	Royal Society for the Protection of Birds
SSSI	Site of Special Scientific Interest
SWLT	Scottish Wild Life Trust

FOREWORD

At the General Assembly of the Church of Scotland in 1984, the Society, Religion and Technology Project was instructed to set up a working party to investigate and report on 'theological and ethical issues in land-use'.

The report now presented commences with some reflections on the theological and ethical issues by the Rev Dr Ruth Page, Lecturer in Systematic Theology, New College, Edinburgh. This is followed by three Chapters which describe major areas of concern and set them in their Scottish context. Chapter 5 gives six examples of different issues and suggests how they have been and how they might be addressed. The following Chapter identifies four questions of critical and immediate importance to the community of Scotland. 'Scotland's responsibility for World Hunger' shows that Scotland as part of Europe has a larger responsibility than simply the giving of aid. Dr Page concludes the report by relating the practical problems of political and social action to an ethical framework.

The Working Party has received information and help from a large number of people. We are particularly grateful to Ian Bainbridge, Rawdon Goodier, Alastair Halbert, Alan Mowle, David Minns, Meredyth Somerville, Howard Wagstaffe and Drenan Watson.

Much of the debate on the use of land is caried out in rather aggressive tones. Some conservationists accuse the farming and foresty communities of philistinism if not of outright vandalism. Some farmers and foresters dismiss their arguments as starry-eyed idealism. In this working party the discussions have been lively but good-tempered. But it would be wrong to expect the report to be based on a consensus. In various sections quite different opinions are set down side by side. It does, however, address itself to central questions that every member believes to be of great importance to the future of Scotland.

There are some omissions. The disposal of nuclear waste is perhaps the most important, particularly in the light of the proposed reprocessing plant at Dounreay. Whatever opinion is held as to the desirability of this development, it is clear that many people in Scotland are concerned about it. The issue demands much fuller treatment than would have been possible in this report.

A number of important parts of Scotland are hardly discussed here, in particular Shetland and Orkney. This is not because of lack of interest, but because it was felt that the special situation of these areas also demands a fuller treatment than we would have been able to give.

There are conflicts of land-use between farming, forestry, 'sporting', nature conservation, tourism, recreation and the needs of the rural and urban communities. Some are genuine, some imagined, some resolvable, some irreconcilable. It is heartening to find that discussion between the different interests is increasing, as is awareness of the underlying questions. The political parties are all beginning to take a more lively interest in the environment, and are beginning to develop policy statements that attempt to grapple with this fundamental but complex subject. But the interest will only be maintained and the policies shaped in a positive way if the community insists on its importance.

We are entering a new period of crisis when major decisions will be made which will have substantial consequences for land-use, for the future of agriculture and of the rural community, and for the inheritance that we leave to our children. If our way of understanding the relationship between humanity and its environment becomes comprehensive and far-sighted rather than confrontational and concerned only with current advantage, then the areas of conflict will diminish and the possibility of creative solutions will increase. If the Report encourages people to develop such attitudes by studying and thinking about the responsible use of land and of our relationship with nature and to recognise it as a matter of ultimate concern, it will have succeeded.

Edinburgh, 1986   CHARLES SOMERVILLE
Working Party Convenor

1. 'THE EARTH IS THE LORD'S'

RESPONSIBLE LAND-USE IN A RELIGIOUS PERSPECTIVE

'The Earth is the Lord's' is a splendid ringing affirmation of the relationship between all creation and its creator. By comparison 'responsible land-use' may seem a dry abstract phrase, applicable only to those with authority for rural decisions and of no particular interest to urban Scots. But this report is written out of the belief that the earth is indeed the Lord's, that it matters how we use it, or let it be used, since we are all accountable to God for what is done with creation. Moreover every Parish is affected by the way land is used, from the purity of its air, to the wholesomeness of food and the possibility of country recreation. City green belts, pollution of waters, pesticides in agriculture, the siting of industrial plants, are only a few of the issues of common concern. Town and country, human and non-human nature are bound together in the 'bundle of life' which is creation. Certainly 'the earth is the Lord's and the fulness thereof', equally certainly we have responsibility under God for the earth and its fulness. The question is how we are to fulfill that responsibility in the light of contemporary problems.

Information and Evaluation

The first requirement is, surely, to be informed concerning the present situation. Stewards who do not know what is happening in their own bailiwick are clearly failing in their responsibility. For that reason, much of this report is concerned with how land is in fact used in Scotland, and how this pattern came to develop. Different interests – economic, recreational, agricultural, conservationist – which go to make up much of the complexity are reviewed and compared. Case studies illustrate particular matters in this country, showing how specific decisions were arrived at, and what was at stake in the clash of interests. Then, because ecological problems occur in worldwide interrelationship (for instance, industrial emissions in Britain contribute 'acid rain' to Norway), there is comment on Scotland's place in relation to land issues in the world at large.

The acquiring of information, then, is a necessary aspect of the Church's responsibility under God for the land in Scotland. But that information has to be evaluated in order to arrive at priorities in each set of circumstances. One example, to which I shall return, is whether a skiing development, with its recreational and tourist benefits, is to be preferred over the conservation of an area of outstanding ecological interest and natural beauty. Decisions in such cases call for ethical as well as informed judgment, so throughout this report moral principles are brought to bear on what has happened or is happening now. It has become increasingly clear to moralists with or without religious persuasion that nature is a candidate for ethical, and not merely utilitarian, judgment. But further, the moral behaviour of Christians derives from their belief in God – here, particularly, belief in God the Creator, on whom everything depends for its existence. This belief is the source and reason for specifically Christian attitudes to the land and its use. Land-use is thus a religious issue. The rest of this Chapter, therefore, will be devoted to sketching out a moral and theological framework which gives a Christian perspective on the status of nature and certain values to guide action in matters of land-use.

Christian attitudes to nature

(a) Instrumental values

It has to be admitted that until recently theology showed little interest in non-human creation. Since the industrial revolution and the population movement to the cities, theology has largely reflected urban preoccupations and emphasised the subjective experience of individuals. Now, however, it has become more concerned with communities – human communities and community with nature. In fact, recent theological interest has been spurred on not only by the evident humanly-wrought devastation of resources, but also by the charge, brought particularly by Lynn White,[1] that the command in Genesis to have dominion over the earth and subdue it, made possible and indeed sanctioned the exploitative attitude. Theologians everywhere leapt to the defence of the Judaeo-Christian tradition. They quoted the many Biblical passages of wonder at nature, invoked figures like St Francis of Assisi and Teilhard de Chardin, and argued (quite fairly) that the mind-set given over to increasingly secular progress rather than obedience to a Biblical precept was to blame for humanity's excesses.

It certainly seems that Lynn White's case was over-stated, but I do not believe that theologians can exculpate their profession so easily. Little was ever written about creation at large, but a recurrent theme in even the briefest treatment has been that nature exists for the benefit of humanity. A very common attitude can be exemplified by quotations from two otherwise rather different theologians in the Reformed Tradition. In his *Commentary on Genesis,* Calvin wrote, 'And hence we infer what was the end for which all things were created; namely, that none of the conveniences and necessaries

[1] For citations here and in the following text of Chapter 1, see *References* (p. 107).

for life might be wanting to men' (p. 96). He was describ-
ing nature before The Fall, but the effect of sin on nature
as Calvin saw it was to make it a more difficult con-
venience to manage. The same utilitarian note was
sounded by John Dickie in 1930. 'The world exists for
our sakes, and not for its own. This follows from the
truth that it is only personal beings capable of responding
to Love that can be objects of Love in the true meaning
of the term. God wills the world therefore as a means,
but only as a means'.

This attitude accords to nature and the inanimate
world – instrumental value – only, since both appear
to exist entirely for the use of men and women. Such
instrumental value in nature is of course extremely important, and we may thank God for it, for without it
humans would not be fed, clothed or sheltered. It is a
value which will appear repeatedly in the report. But
when the sheer usefulness of nature to humanity is given
overriding priority in attitudes and actions it encourages
the masterfulness of an anthropocentric and utilitarian
view of all that is not human. There would be nothing in
this attitude on its own to inhibit use to the point of
exploitation. A further corollary is that what is not of use
has no worth and is therefore negligible or dispensable.
From this point of view, nature has no standing of its
own before humanity or before God, and no independent
right to consideration apart from, at best, the preservation of its usefulness.

Recently, that sense of the need for preservation for
future generations has become more acute in the
Western World, although it is a hard message for countries with a young and insecure economy to bear.

Where it can be enforced, a conservation policy may
serve to curb short-sighted utilitarian practices like the
depleting of fish stocks. Nevertheless, much damage has
already been done. 'The Scottish Highlands provide an

example of a man-made wet desert; a long history of erosion resulting from deforestation and sheep-farming have led to ecological stagnation' (Black, p. 6). This is not quoted in order to apportion blame for one cannot always foresee the results of one's actions, but to illustrate from our own country the practical dangers of an exclusively utilitarian approach, however important the instrumental value of creation continues to be. Moreover, from a theological point of view, in the instrumental approach 'Creation is merged with providence and virtually disappears behind it' (Hendry, p. 17). To bring it back into view creation as such and not only its providential aspect will have to be valued. One approach to this was given by Moltmann in his 1985 *Gifford Lectures,* when he pointed out that the pinnacle of creation in *Genesis I* was not the making of man, but the day God rested, when all creation was living together. Therefore, as one practical need is to give non-human nature moral standing in decisions on land-use, so one theological need is to see all created things in their own relation to their Creator rather than as 'conveniences and necessaries' for humanity and nothing more.

(b) Inherent value

Throughout the Bible there is a prominent strand of awe or wonder at nature as something to be contemplated and considered (the heavens, the lilies) since their beauty and order is expressive of their Creator. This illustrates a second kind of value, inherent value, in creation. There are aesthetic connotations here, for inherent value is something paintings, for instance, are said to have since their contents give pleasure, satisfaction or enlargement of vision. This is still human-centred, in that men and women are those finding or failing to find value. But the values are those of appreciation rather than use. In this way, to give a very different quotation from Calvin, nature is 'the theatre of the glory of God'. Thus Torridon or the Kyles of Bute may have inherent value, as may a well-ploughed field, in the pleasure and satisfaction it gives. An ecological system with balance among its interrelated species has the same kind of beauty too. This value finds its place in the report, because the inherent value of a site may now be a factor in decisions on land-use. Lord Ashby, for instance, recommends putting a Suffolk landscape into the same category as a painting of the landscape by Constable, and acting accordingly. Just as the painting should be preserved, so should the landscape. He goes on to argue for the preservation of species and environment because 'they are unique, or irreplaceable, or simply part of the fabric of civilisation' also '[because] we do not understand how they have acquired their durability and what all the consequences would be if we destroyed them' (p. 85). Further, from a religious point of view the consideration of inherent value means bearing in mind the beauty or the fulness of variety in creation (what theologians like Augustine called its 'plenitude') when the extinction of a species or the spoliation of land is at issue.

(c) Intrinsic value

There is no great controversy over affirming that non-human nature has instrumental and inherent value. But there has been less willingness to attribute to it intrinsic value, that is, a value of its own quite independent of human judgment on its use or beauty. Value, after all, has often been thought of as value to someone's consciousness. But this view has its dangers in putting all the emphasis on people who value, since it could lead to the inference that only the interests of articulate valuers have value. In that case, for instance, the interests of an infant who could express no values would not be considered in a moral judgment. Further, Peter Singer has argued in *Animal Liberation* that non-human animals have interests even though they cannot express values as humans can. They know pain and pleasure, and require shelter, food and the chance to reproduce. Attfield extends this upholding of interests in a modified form to plants, though not to inanimate nature which he holds as inherent value only (p. 153). If plants and animals are seen to have interests of their own, they acquire a moral standing analogous to the standing of a human infant, and although they cannot represent their own interests in human decisions on land-use, their moral standing has to be considered independently of human preferences and purposes. Singer proposes the principle that 'the interests of every being affected by an action are to be taken into account and given the same weight as the like interests of any other being'. (Singer 1980, cited by Attfield p. 166.) From that point of view, plants and animals have intrinsic value on moral grounds and this is reflected in the report whenever their good, which may not be identical to human good, is given full consideration.

The debate on the standing of non-human nature has for the most part taken place among moral philosophers with an ecological bent. But its results can be adopted and even expanded by the Church. The quotation from John Dickie (given earlier) discounted the intrinsic value of what is not human on the grounds that only persons can respond to, and hence be the real objects of, love. But such a view seems both to underestimate plants and animals and to limit the Creator in his relationship with all creation. It means, moreover, that God would have had no relationship of real love with creation during all the thousands of millenia of evolution before humanity appeared; this, surely, is unduly anthropocentric. If God is the generative ground of 'all things visible and invisible', then he is the ultimate source of these interests which are now recognised to raise plants and animals to moral standing. Presumably they always had such standing in God's sight. The range of interests and capacity for response may be less in most other species than it is in most humans, but they responded 'after their kind' in their development and interrelationship.

Certainly a personal relationship is the best and highest we know as personal beings, but God may relate in far higher ways than we can imagine from our limited human viewpoint. Even to relate to humans, therefore, is kindly self-limitation on God's part so that relating to non-human creation is only, as it were, more of the same action. Moreover, we respond to plants and animals as humans and hence limited in our understanding by our otherness from them. Such limitation cannot be projected onto God who relates directly and in the best possible way to every aspect of creation. He is a God who knows when sparrows fall to the ground (Matthew 10:29) and what it is for sparrows to fall to the ground.

Further, just as God desires good for his human creation, so he desires good for what is not human. On this ground alone Christians can claim intrinsic value for plants, animals and even rocks, since their standing derives from the value they have to their Creator. Nature 'exists for God's glory', that is to say, it has a meaning and worth beyond its meaning and worth as seen from the point of view of human utility. It is in this sense that we can say it has an intrinsic value (Montefiore p.67). Natural evil such as earthquakes or floods for example, does not affect this value any more than the sin of moral evil affects humanity's value to God, but it does observe the relationship. In humanity's dealings with non-human creation, therefore, we are involved with others which have their own good, and a value above and beyond their benefits to humanity.

Christian relationships with nature

(a) Steward

Given, then, that land-use concerns the instrumental, inherent and intrinsic value of what is not human, how should men and women behave, and what recommendations can the Church make? Theology at this point cannot of itself give prescriptions for behaviour in every case. For instance, to revert to an earlier example, it cannot on its own decide between a skiing development and the retention of land for conservation. What has been argued thus far, however, does show that conservation has a real case for the Church to ponder, which is neither romantic nor obscurantist and can be weighed against both the benefits and the harm of the skiing proposal. Moreover, theological reflection does not provide roles for the Church to adopt towards non-human nature in the total scheme of creation. I have chosen three which cohere with the three kinds of values, although in practice both the values and the roles are likely to be blended. In these roles some actions will become impossible and out of character; others may be judged by the degree to which they express the relationship in action. But again, it must be said that these roles do not give precise rules. Instead, they describe the nature of the relationships within which action ought to take place.

The first and best-known of these roles is that of 'steward', which has had a long and often honourable history in the church, to describe humanity's relationship with nature in its instrumental aspect. At its best, this has meant that as stewards of the land, people were 'responsible for its conservation, for its lasting improvement and also for the care of our fellow creatures, its non-human inhabitants' (Attfield p. 45). The role emphasises that the earth is not ours to possess or manipulate at will, but that we hold it under tenure, so to speak, with a delegated responsibility. Humanity is accountable to God for what happens on earth, but at the same time the relationship between humanity and nature echoes on the creaturely level the providential role traditionally ascribed to God in the government and preservation of creation. Some actions do become impossible when the role of steward is taken seriously: anything which could be deemed exploitation; the exhaustion of resources; making present profitability the sole effective criterion; exporting rather than solving problems; allowing bad situations to become worse through sheer lack of concern. This still leaves a great deal to be decided, such as the point at which use becomes exploitation, or the appropriate action when the best for one piece of creation can be achieved only at the expense of another. Yet it does show the kind of responsible relationship within which answers are to be sought.

(c) Trustee

The inherent value of nature, the beauty of the way creation is and how it works together, suggests a variant of the stewardship role for humanity, that of 'trustee'. The model here is of trustees for an art gallery or a Deacons' Court entrusted with maintaining the fabric of church buildings. God is thus seen to have given to humanity the trust of maintaining the fabric of creation. It is a large part of the trustees' job to conserve works of art, which may mean cleaning and restoring as well as keeping them in being and allowing them to be enjoyed. Just so, conservation of what there is, or what still remains, is part of Christian trusteeship under God. The trustees may not themselves appreciate all the art which is under their care and may have to be informed by experts that 'this is good and worth preserving'. Similarly, humanity may not feel instant appreciation of obscure insects or the ecological system of a peat bog, yet may be told by experts that 'this is rare, beautiful in its own way and worth preserving'. Such direction has to be taken seriously by trustees under God of the inherent, and even more of the intrinsic value of nature.

It is a further role of trustees to conserve for the sake of future generations and that is also an important aspect of our God-given responsibility. Stewards likewise hand on their area of responsibility to their successors. Concern for the future is an urgent incentive to action. As John Black emphasises, 'The essence of the "ecological crisis" is not that we are ruining our environment; it is that by ruining our environment we are imperilling our own future' (p. 12). Attfield, moreover, makes it a basic aim for all environmental ethics that each generation should leave the world at least no more polluted than it found it (Ch. 6, pp. 88-110). It is not surprising, therefore, that future effects figure largely in the report, so that one of the matters for Church members to decide is what action it should take as steward and trustee, under God, for the conservation of the resources of Scotland for the future. Action which is ruled out by the trustee relationship with creation is the perpetration or condoning of vandalism towards nature in all forms of human ugliness, from litter to graceless building, to industrial waste. (From this point of view, for instance, what is ruled in by trusteeship is encouragement for the grassing over of old pit bings.) What is impossible for a trustee, is the careless breaking-up of ecological balance in the country, an act comparable to allowing a delicate machine to lose components necessary to its working.

Stewards and trustees are active guardians and conscious encouragers of the land. These roles emphasise the difference between humans and all the rest of creation, with the responsibility that brings, and they reflect nature in its providential forms of usefulness and beauty. But the doctrine of creation is not to be merged with belief in providence to the extent that it disappears as a separate consideration, nor is humanity altogether of a different origin in kind from the nature it superintends. What is needed in the third role, therefore, is an expression of humanity as itself as an evolved species relating to other species which have their own intrinsic value.

(c) Companion

Such a role is provided by the model of companionship. That can express natural and human interdependence without excluding the distinctiveness of each, for companions are involved together in whatever they may be doing, yet retain their own identities in the process. Dependence and independence coexist in a healthy companionship just as humanity is dependent on its natural environment but is also a unique species with its own independent capacity. Conversely, companionship expresses the dependence of the natural world upon humanity's stewardship while simultaneously emphasising the irreplaceability and intrinsic value of each species. Moreover, companions are those who share space or a journey; there is an element of 'being in this together' in the relationship. Similarly, the 'ecological crisis' is not a crisis in non-human nature; we are in this together, and if we are to get out, it will again be together. Moltmann uses a similar motif of 'fellowship' with creation. Dwelling on Christ's coming to serve rather than be served, he writes, 'And he served in order to make us for fellowship with God and openness for one another. In the light of Christ's mission Genesis 1:28 will have to be interpreted . . . not "subdue the earth", but "free the earth through fellowship with it".' (1979, p. 129.)

Those who have written out of the so-called 'deep' ecological movement express the same sense of fellowship in the entire 'biosphere', or what J. E. Lovelock has called 'Gaia', the whole being of Earth. There could be a danger in this breadth of outlook that the 'biosphere', (like any other totality) might come to be regarded as more important than the welfare of individual members of the 'biotic community' (the terms are Aldo Leopold's). Yet conceptions like 'biosphere' or 'Gaia' express a sense of wholeness which is more than a mere sum of parts and give a vision of the possibilities of creation in our corner of the universe. The biotic community will not be realized in its fulness until the eschaton, the end when all tensions and dislocations are finally resolved in God, and the 'lion will lie down with the lamb'. But fellowship, companionship and community exercised now, however imperfectly, is a response to the Creator of the whole biosphere.

The role of companion excludes the possibility of adversarial tactics with nature – that attitude of confrontation and control which was thought until recently to be an essential part of 'the scientific method'. Instead, companionship involves a dialogue to-and-fro between humanity's interest and nature's. There is a sense in which companionship thus exercised is a fulfilment of the command to love our neighbours as ourselves – our neighbours in this case being our neighbourhood, our environment. The existence of that relationship prevents any powerful takeover on the part of humanity. Humans can defend themselves from nature's advances, but nature cannot defend itself so well from humans, so the necessity for respect inherent in companionship is a requirement of humanity alone. This is the same respect that God shows to all creation as he 'companions' it, but does not overwhelm it with his power.

Steward, Trustee, Companion

The roles shade into each other and all are necessary for a balanced relationship with what is not human since each role carries a range of connotations, some of which are not suitable. Stewardship, for instance, may connote everything from the encouragement of nature to its domination. At one end of the range it has business management and even lordly connotations of power which are undesirable since these reflect the attitudes which have produced the crisis. What is required is a view of stewardship tempered by companionship so that it is more co-operative than domineering. On the other hand, companionship on its own could be construed as a relationship which is too gentle to take the hard decisions which have to be made in situations of competing interests. In that case, it needs the judgment involved in stewardship to make it viable. The unwelcome connotation of trusteeship is that passive unprofitable preservation which was rebuked in Jesus' parable of the talents. It requires the warmth of companionship and the activity of stewardship to make it an attractive role. Just as the values that nature has merged together and may all be found in one situation, so the roles of humanity in relation to creation have to inform and balance each other.

'If Christianity will be shown in the end to have failed the world, it will have failed because it encouraged man to set himself apart from the rest of nature, or, at the very least, because it failed to discourage him from doing so.' (Black, p. 121.) This is John Black's warning against Christian unconcern over the concentration of ecological problems and potential disasters which have accumulated through careless and selfish land-use, some of which are documented in this report. It is, as I have said, a religious issue concerning God's world. But the Church may feel that although it has an interest, it has no voice in these matters, since the State has largely taken over responsibility for industry, planning, amenity, wildlife and landscape. Most of the difficult decisions between, say, social benefits and industrial profitability are made by Government. Yet any government in a democracy has a duty to 'the public good', a duty to society. But, as Black comments, 'Duty to society is a nebulous concept, interpretable only in terms of the decisions of that society' (p. 88). Thus, if society is prepared to countenance the exploitation of resources, there is nothing to stop policies which could end only in their depletion, if not exhaustion. It is only where a significant, vocal and active section of society which has its own frame of reference (as Christians have their sense of responsibility to God for creation) expresses its priorities for policies, that the Government, which has the executive power, may be moved to act accordingly. This is not a simple matter, but it is not impossible either, and is a part the Church should play. The Church itself contains many interests and diverse points of view, yet these can be held together on this issue by the affirmation that this is God's world which is valuable to Him and hence must be cared for as something with its own intrinsic value.

> Let the heavens be glad, and let the earth rejoice;
> let the sea roar, and all that fills it;
> let the field exult, and everything in it!
> Then shall all the trees of the wood sing for joy
> before the Lord, for he comes
> for he comes to judge the earth.
> He will judge the world with righteousness,
> and the peoples with his truth.
>
> *(Psalm 96:11-13)*

2. WORLD CONSERVATION AND THE UK RESPONSE

Man has tended to use natural resources in a profligate way throughout history, always moving into virgin lands, heedless of problems of erosion, of pollution, of the destruction of nature, of the welfare of existing communities. The consequences have ranged from dust bowls in America to dead, stinking rivers and lakes in industrial Europe, from the disappearance of the Caledonian forest to the desertification of once fertile Mediterranean lands.

Public concern about conservation has a history dating back at least to the Victorian age. Since the Second World War, however, there has been a rapid increase in understanding of the scale and nature of environmental issues in a technological age and with it a belief that the problems that man has created could be solved by man. The optimism is hardly justified by results so far. In 1962 Rachel Carson brought to the world's notice the effect of DDT as it accumulates at the higher levels of the food chain. Although DDT was banned, it is still used in some parts of the world. The *Nuclear Test Ban Treaty* (1963) followed the realisation of the deadly effects of radiation. While important in stopping massive pollution from atmospheric tests, it has by no means solved the problem of radiation.

In 1972 there was a major advance in international consciousness of environmental questions when the United Nations Conference on the Human Environment was held at Stockholm. This was the first attempt to bring together the wide range of problems of international concern. Since then the international debate has widened substantially, addressing a range of gigantic issues; the desperate problems of hunger, in particular in Africa;

the successes and failures of the Green revolution; the exploitation of virgin forests; the use of arable land for cash crops in poor countries; the wholesale destruction of top soil through erosion and pollution.

In 1980 a *World Conservation Strategy* was published by three international conservation agencies. This propounded the vital necessity of conservation for sustained development. The requirements for achieving this were set out with suggested priorities for national and international action. The main thrust of the Strategy was towards those parts of the world where the ecological base is fragile.

By 1983 the major conservation bodies of the UK had together produced a long and detailed response, *The Conservation and Development Programme of the UK* which attempts to develop the themes of the strategy in terms of an industrial society in a temperate zone. It stresses the importance of environmental education and suggests that an ethical code as a basis for environmental decisions might be developed.

Since the end of the War the UK has taken several important steps to deal with pollution, in particular the clean air legislation and the reduction of pollution in rivers. The *Town and Country Planning Act* (1947) marked the introduction of comprehensive control of development. The present system of local and structure plans was introduced in 1972. From the point of view of land use these measures have been reasonably successful in containing urban sprawl and sporadic development in rural areas but in practice 'Town and Country' planning is urban. There is no planning control over changes of rural land-use and very little over the erection of agricultural buildings.

The *Wild Life and Countryside Act* (1981) consolidated and developed earlier legislation concerning nature conservation. For the first time it included provisions for compensation to landowners who are being prevented from developing land for agricultural use.

Growing awareness of the urgent need for conservation measures is illustrated on the one hand by the establishment, since the War, of Government agencies charged with wildlife and countryside conservation, and on the other by a variety of voluntary organisations dedicated to these ends.

The Government organisations operating in Scotland are the Nature Conservancy Council and the Countryside Commission for Scotland. The former covers the whole of Great Britain, but has separate Scottish, English and Welsh headquarters, that for Scotland being in Edinburgh. Its role in the protection of wildlife through the designation of National Nature Reserves and the notification of Sites of Special Scientific Interest is further considered here in Chapter 4(c) pp. 41-44. In addition it has the task of advising national and local government on conservation matters, and of promoting awareness of conservation objectives among the public.

The Countryside Commission for Scotland was established in 1968 and like its sister Commission in England and Wales, is concerned with providing and improving facilities for the enjoyment of the countryside and with conserving and improving its natural beauty and amenity. In conjunction with The Scottish Office, the Commission was instrumental in the designation of National Scenic Areas and it collaborates with Local Authorities in setting up Country Parks and Regional Parks. There are no National Parks in Scotland.

Effective conservation management depends heavily on the results of scientific research. Both the Government-funded organisations mentioned above can, to different extents, carry out appropriate surveys and research, and may also commission research for example from the Institute of Terrestial Ecology (Natural

Environment Research Council), or from the Universities. The ITE is represented in Scotland by laboratories at Edinburgh and Banchory, and in addition to commissioned research also carries out its own investigations bearing on the ecology of land use, problems of pollution, acid rain and other questions.

Numerous thriving voluntary organisations concern themselves with the conservation of wildlife and the countryside, or with other non-commercial uses of land. These include old-established bodies like the National Trust for Scotland and the Royal Society for the Protection of Birds, while in the past twenty-five years several other groups have come on the scene, of which one of the most active is the Scottish Wild Life Trust (established 1964). The above named organisations all maintain reserves of varying size. Other societies, such as Friends of the Earth (Scotland), are predominantly pressure groups, seeking to spread the message of conservation and environmental protection, both among the public and with Government at all levels. A rather different and very recent development of considerable significance is the spread of Farming, Forestry and Wildlife Advisory Groups (FFWAGS). These now exist in several Scottish Regions and draw together those concerned with such activities, seeking to promote practices which allow wildlife conservation to co-exist with the productive use of land. Some FFWAGS employ full time officers to advise farmers and foresters on conservation.

While the existence of all these active organisations ensures that major issues of conservation are debated, it is unfortunately true that Scotland's political and administrative system produces a fragmented approach to questions of land-use. A number of different bodies may be involved in a single issue, all representing a special interest. Agriculture, forestry, nature conservation, tourism, planning are all administered through separate structures.

It has been suggested that healthy competition between different forms of land-use is the best way of achieving a proper economic balance. There may have been some truth in this in the past, although the record of history is not convincing. In the new situation it seems unlikely to be the best administrative framework to develop integrated policies of land-use.

TABLE 2:1

Nature Reserves and Parks

	Approx Number	Approx Area (hectares)
Nature Conservancy Council:		
National Nature Reserves*	63	100527
SSSI's*	1075	604330
National Trust for Scotland: Countryside properties	90	44450
Royal Society for the Protection of Birds: Reserves*	40	22500
Scottish Wild Life Trust: Reserves*	72	16500
Countryside Commission for Scotland:		
National Scenic Areas (12% of total land surface)		1010500
Local Authorities: Country Parks	33	5756

* leased, owned or managed.

It will be noted that the primary role of most conservation organisations is to preserve areas of the land and their natural inhabitants. This is an admirable intention but it is unfortunate that in the popular mind 'conservation' is thought of only as 'nature conservation', and mainly as the preservation of threatened species of bird, animal or plant. The concept of 'resource conservation' is less well understood. We need to care for the fundamental resources of soil, air and water now, and in a sustainable future in the interests of the whole living community, plant, animal and human.

3. THE SCOTTISH LANDSCAPE

Nature and man have combined in forming the landscape of Scotland. The basic physiographic divisions of the Highlands, South Uplands and Central Lowlands disguise a wide variety of landscapes. Although the highest point is only 1343 metres above sea level, Scotland is an upland country with about sixty-five per cent of the land surface above 120 metres and, because of the juxtaposition of lowland and upland, has an overall mountainous appearance.

Situated off the North West coast of Europe on the same latitude as south Alaska, it is only the presence of the North Atlantic Current which permits agriculture in these northern islands. The influence of the ocean is all pervasive in a small country with a deeply indented coastline of some 3700 kilometres where few places are more than 60 kilometres from salt water. But Scotland faces the North Sea as well as the Atlantic Ocean and this contrast is pronounced in the difference between the climate of the east and the west, accentuated by the basic division into highland and lowland.

The West of Scotland has an equable, damp climate and a high rainfall (100-150 centimetres on the Atlantic coast, rising to 250 centimetres or more per year on the mountains), with temperatures generally higher than in the east, particularly in winter. Along the east coast rainfall may be less than 75 centimetres per year and summer drought is common, while temperature extremes are more frequent than in the west, with severe frosts in winter. Sunshine levels are generally higher in the east.

Such a climate imposes constraints on production from the land, which vary with geographical position, altitude and exposure. Moreover there have been marked changes of climate in the past which have affected patterns of land-use, while short-term fluctuations in weather regimes always reduce the stability of yields in locations which are marginal for agriculture. Over much of Scotland up to altitudes of 6-800 metres, the present climate would support a cover of native forest, in the absence of human occupation. South of the Highland boundary fault and in the glens and parts of the west coast this would consist of deciduous woodland; to the north and west pine and birch would predominate. Such forest certainly clothed the landscape in former times, but most of it was cleared, partly for fuel (charcoal) and timber for building, partly to create building land. On the more fertile soils grassland has replaced forest, while on the poorer acidic soils heather moors became widespread in drier areas, wet grass moors or blanket bog in the wetter west and north. Today only about 12 per cent of the land surface is tree-covered, and much of this is plantation. Elsewhere tree regeneration is largely prevented by grazing and burning. On the relatively well drained and fertile soils bracken has often invaded and spread.

The land-use pattern evolved slowly as man came to occupy the country. Population growth was slow and had only reached 1.27 millions in 1755 when Alexander Webster used parish ministers as the statistical source for his census of the population, most of whom were rural and half of whom were in northern Scotland. During the nineteenth century, however, as in the rest of Great Britain, there were significant changes; by the mid-point the population had grown to 2.9 million and the rural population was down to 42 per cent. The drift to the towns had begun and, particularly in northern Scotland, depopulation was becoming significant. Today, the distribution of population is very uneven, with four-fifths concentrated in the central belt.

Agrarian change at this time also started to form the Scottish landscape as we know it today. Dykes enclosed field systems which still exist, extensive drainage schemes were begun, woodland was planted and pastures and crop rotation developed. Social change also followed, with straths in the Highlands cleared for sheep farming; surveyors laid out the estates and the ownership of the land altered from the common holding to the formation of large estates.

The most striking feature of agriculture in Scotland is the small area which is capable of intense cultivation, with the best farmed land stretching up the east coast from the English border to the Moray coast and extending into the Orkney Islands. Nearly half the country is described as rough grazing; cattle, either for dairying or beef, and sheep predominate in appropriate areas according to the topography and climate. In the Highlands and Islands there is an indistinct line between living off the land and off the sea. The unique crofting system, which is an hereditary one where small patches of tillable land are combined with common grazing on the hill, evolved in response to population pressure and economic conditions. It is essentially part-time employment and must be supplemented by other income.

The pattern of land-use has altered greatly since the Second World War. The traditional system of agriculture gave way to mechanisation and the use of chemical fertilisers and pesticides. In some of the arable areas stock has been reduced, barley replaced oats as the staple crop, much of it for animal feeding in the upland areas where higher stocking levels are becoming common. Afforestation has been a prominent feature in the upland areas and the face of parts of the countryside has changed complexion under a cover of conifers. Urban and road expansion has nibbled away at high quality land, particularly in the Central Lowlands, while the growth of recreation and tourism has placed pressure on areas which are often ecologically fragile. At the same time, the decline of coal mining and heavy industries has released land for redevelopment in the most populated areas.

Scotland remains a rural country and 98 per cent of it has been designated as countryside by the Countryside Commission. It is fortunate in being not only self-sufficient in beef and mutton, potatoes, barley and milk, but, with 2.5 million cows and 7.5 million sheep, also has exportable surpluses of meat. The total annual value of farming is approximately one-thousand million pounds per annum, with 70 per cent coming from animal products, 25 per cent from crops and most of the remainder from horticulture. Employment on the land has fallen, but the capital investment has markedly increased since 1945. Land-use policies have not changed greatly in the arable areas, but the system of farming based on intensive cropping with chemical controls has given rise to concern about a sustainable future.

On the uplands, however, radical changes and increasingly competitive claims require the intelligent co-operation of various bodies and interests if the welfare of the community as a whole is to be served and resources are not to be depleted. Hill farming, stalking and shooting are now faced with the demands of forestry, winter sports, tourism and wildlife conservation. Easier access to, and greater comprehension of, the value of the country and its scenery create further pressures.

It is vital that the last true wilderness areas should be preserved; it is essential to sustain those areas where mankind and nature have combined to produce a satisfying landscape, and it is also vital that those areas which have degenerated through man's action over the years should be rehabilitated.

4. LAND-USE

(a) Arable Farming

Success Story

Since the early 1950s there has been a revolution in arable farming systems. On the one hand, it can be said to have been a success story. Productivity has increased by 75 per cent, measured by output; the UK now has a surplus in cereals, and the percentage of personal income spent on food in the UK has dropped. It is often said that agriculture has responded to the needs of the community with a vigour unmatched by other industries. Standards of management of the new systems, productivity, and relationships with the advisory services have all been of a high order.

The new problem of surpluses

Before the War Britain imported two thirds of its food, mainly from countries within the Empire. Vigorous efforts during the War reduced this dependence on temperate foodstuffs to 50 per cent. After the War it was broadly accepted by all political parties that agricultural policies should be developed to make the UK much more self-sufficient in food. European Economic Community (EEC) policy makers had the same end in view and believed that a balance could be achieved in most temperate products in the 1960s. Britain's entry into the EEC postponed this and surpluses are only now developing. Steps to deal with agricultural over-production are now being fiercely debated. Already a milk quota scheme has been introduced. Cereal support prices have been reduced and although further reductions are being proposed, they are being fought, especially by West Germany. The introduction of a quota scheme has also been strongly canvassed. Problems of the working and cost of the Common Agricultural Policy (CAP) are so serious as to endanger the future of the Community. As well as the tension within the Community, the present policies have produced a threat of a trade war with the USA, incensed at the availability of vast amounts of grain on the world market at heavily subsidised rates, (it will be appreciated that US grain is also subsidised).

The arable revolution

The main factors in the post-war revolution in arable farming have been:

(1) the universal adoption of mechanisation, such as tractors, combines;
(2) the inevitable consequent reduction of the labour force, by 50 per cent since the 1930s;
(3) the increased use of chemicals, fertilisers, pesticides and fungicides;
(4) change in crops grown, for instance, much increased acreage of barley, reduction of oats, disappearance of sugar beet, introduction of oil seed rape;
(5) improved seed varieties (short straw, early ripening); increased use of silage;
(6) more uniform systems and standards of farming. Critics have said that farming has become 'follow the instructions printed on the bag';
(7) a large proportion of barley goes for intensive stock rearing. Although more land is under cultivation, stock totals have increased.

Some consequences

There have been important consequences of the drive for productivity and the consequent dependence on high input farming. 'High input' is taken to mean farming with a substantial capital investment in machinery, high energy-consumption and substantial use of agrochemicals.

(1) As in every other industry, mechanisation has resulted in a reduction in employment.

(2) Although, on the whole, Scotland has not been afflicted by 'prairie farming', and field systems established early in the nineteenth century have largely been retained, there has been considerable destruction of broad-leaved woodland and long established hedgerows. One estimate claims that 25 per cent of all hedgerows in lowland Scotland have been pulled out in the last forty years.

(3) New seed varieties have proved susceptible to disease, therefore requiring more spraying. Some are now developed as a package of seed, with its own back-up of chemical sprays and fertilisers.

(4) Mixed arable/stock farming in the traditional pattern is reduced. The use of rotation as a pivotal feature of good husbandry has been largely abandoned.

(5) Although much less serious than in England, the disposal of straw has become a problem.

Support for the present system

Proponents believe that the systems are sustainable and deny that substantial damage is being done to the environment. They would describe modern systems as following the normal practices of good husbandry but using manufactured fertilisers which provide precisely the same major nutrients as animal manures. The increase of fertility raises the general level of biological activity, weeds grow faster, pathogens and parasites flourish. More available feed allows higher stocking levels but again, encourages animal pathogens and parasites. This competitive activity has to be dealt with selectively and powerful tools in the shape of herbicides, fungicides and insecticides are available. Some disease resistant crop varieties have also been introduced. New problems have emerged of which the best known was with DDT. Stringent controls, legal and voluntary, have been developed to try to avoid similar problems, but resistance to other products has developed, and the search for new more effective substances has tended to be continuous. It remains to be seen whether totally different and absolutely safe ways of controlling the competition can be developed. These systems have allowed farmers to translate increased fertility into higher productivity.

Fertilisers and pesticides have maintained fertility and control better than rotations and have allowed continuous cropping. Many arable farmers have found cattle and sheep unnecessary and the hedges that contained them, disposable. It should be noted that in Scotland many arable farms still retain some stock although not necessarily in the interests of maintaining a traditional rotation.

Criticism of present systems

There is a body of informed opinion which is concerned about the long-term viability of a system of high input farming. The arguments can be summarised as follows:

(1) Recent research has commented on the dearth of information on the effects of heavy applications of nitrogenous fertilisers on soil fauna with regard both to soil fertility and pest populations. In some circumstances this has tended to decrease the diversity and size of populations of most groups of soil invertebrates, particularly earthworms. However, there may be compensatory effects, such as greater crop yields, leaving more plant residues to provide food for soil invertebrates. It is also suggested that pesticides may change the delicate balance between organisms. There are claims that yields

can only be increased or even maintained by larger inputs of fertiliser and that this is likely to produce serious long-term effects on the soil. There is a need for substantial, properly directed research under UK conditions.

(2) Use of weed-killers, pesticides and fungicides is indiscriminate and to a certain extent cannot be controlled. Resistance is built up and higher inputs have to be used. Wildlife and vegetation on land surrounding the sprayed areas are affected.

(3) Present high energy inputs may become uneconomic.

(4) Productivity has been measured as yield per hectare. If measured against various inputs, increases have not been achieved. Since 1950 the use of fertilisers has increased by 700 per cent, pesticides and fungicides by 650 per cent, energy by 250 per cent and capital input by 350 per cent.

(5) Concern has been expressed about run-off or leaching of fertilisers – into rivers and lochs, but there is no hard evidence that this is yet a major problem in Scotland.

Future policy

The debate about the future is wide ranging. Many farmers believe that present systems are sustainable and, given satisfactory changes in the CAP and UK Government policies, they see future patterns as modifications of present conditions rather than radical changes of direction. Farmers are concerned that systems to deal with surpluses – whether by supporting price reductions, quotas or other schemes – may result in such an economic squeeze that small family farms in particular will be forced out of business, and this may have a serious effect on the prosperity of the rural community. So they support and are engaged in a vigorous search for alternative crops such as oil-seed-rape. There is much interest in integrating farming with low ground forestry, both conifers and broadleaved (deciduous) trees. Recently an improved scheme of grants for planting broadleaved trees has been introduced but the long term cycle required is financially difficult to establish. There is an awareness of conservation problems but it is considered that satisfactory solutions can be reached (for example, the introduction of strict legislation on the use of sprays is supported by the industry nationally).

Another approach suggests that the problem of European surpluses in many major products could be treated as an opportunity to re-examine fundamental assumptions in farming methods and to develop creative alternatives rather than to propose the imposition of negative cuts and quotas. This proposes the development of lower input farming systems; systems which use the minimum inputs of capital and agrochemicals. Considerable research has been done in the USA, Switzerland and the Netherlands into such systems but practically none in the UK. The reasons for the lack of interest are firstly, the drive for increased productivity at all costs and secondly, the good fortune of the UK in having a less fragile environment so that the pressures of intensive farming have been less apparent.

The consideration of low input farming should start not at the end of the production line but from a study of the ecosystem in all its complexity. Lower input systems will make higher demands on management, require a higher labour input, have a significantly lower output, but would use less energy and other resources. Changeover raises substantial problems of management, finance and profitability either for single farms or for a larger movement, and could only be achieved with substantial financial support. Before any judgement of the viability of low or lower input farming can be made, it is essential that research should be initiated in the agricultural colleges and elsewhere into a whole range of questions, of management (particularly of transition), of varieties of plant and breeds of animals, of possible yields of different products and varying inputs.

Arable farming is at a turning point, and finding the future direction is vital to the whole community. The decisions made will have important implications for those parts of Scotland where it is practised, but also in other areas which are likely to feel the effect of major changes in the systems adopted in the more fertile parts of the country.

(b) The Uplands

Agriculture, forestry, game management (deer and grouse) and nature conservation are the four cardinal uses of the uplands. Tourism and recreation are very important but they do not raise such fundamental issues in terms of land-use and management, except in relatively small areas, or where they bring about special effects due to the concentration of large numbers of people.

Too often the different uses are seen to be mutually antagonistic and this is encouraged by administrative systems that have evolved. The priorities required if responsible land use is to be achieved demand a long timescale to redress the damage of the past and to establish the principles of resource conservation. Such policies have to be evolved and established not only by political and fiscal action but through discussion and co-operation of the whole community, particularly the local community. The Scottish Uplands have great diversity and sensible land-use policies must vary to suit the variety of environments.

Grazing of large animals such as sheep, deer and sometimes cattle is a potent factor in the ecology of that large area of mainly natural grassland, heather and a variety of non-woodland plant assemblages which dominates the Border hills, most of the Highlands and the

Western Isles. The great part of what is now open grazing was at one time forest or scrub except on the highest ground and in the most exposed situations. The Border hills have been sheep pasture for many centuries, but the demise of the forest in the Highlands passed through its final stages only within the last two hundred years.

The comparatively stable and fertile soils of the Border hills have sustained heavy grazing without serious destructive effects. In parts of the Highlands, on the other hand, especially where soil fertility is very poor, and where the peat lies directly on the rock, there is a very different picture. For example in the north west, the combination of burning and excessive grazing has caused the erosion of peat, exposing the underlying rock or scree. Ecologists have often been vocal in condemning land-use systems based on extensive grazing where farmers and landowners have failed to acknowledge and make provision for the delicate equilibrium of the Highlands. For the individual farmer, however, it seems that the problem is too deeply seated for him to resolve unaided.

A system of inappropriate stocking of grazing animals combined with muirburn can destroy fragile habitats, the end result being soil erosion. Under more judicious use the destruction of a part of the vegetation cover may be only temporary because the fundamental productivity of the site remains unimpared. Ensuring that such productivity is maintained is the essence of resource conservation in an economic framework and should be the prime responsibility of those who have control of range use, whether for the purposes of grazing by sheep, deer, or forestry.

The increasing economic pressure on hill farming, the expansion of afforestation and the growing interest in nature conservation all point to the need for more research into new forms of land management. Despite the advances made in all these types of land-use new knowledge is needed in how to develop ecologically more balanced systems, based on a better understanding of the main components and acknowledging the different priorities, ecological and economic, that should guide land-use.

There are some areas where the needs of nature conservation should be paramount, while in others there will be a single form of economic activity, but between these extremes balanced systems of land-use must be adopted. On the other hand there are large areas of the uplands and highlands where grazing or browsing animals will continue to play a prominent role whatever land-use system is adopted.

Hill farming

The future of hill farming has to be considered from many aspects, but resource conservation must be fundamental. There are areas of Scotland where injudicious burning and over concentration on sheep, has led to severe deterioration of the grazing value of the vegetation. It is a matter of urgency that policies should be developed to halt this deterioration of the environment and initiate the long, slow process of rehabilitation. It has been suggested that some Highland areas could be more profitable and productive if the extensive system of free range sheep farming was replaced by more intensive management in limited areas, leaving the high ground to deer and other wildlife. Alternatively, experiments have in some cases suggested that lower sheep stocking rates with the introduction or increase of cattle can produce a substantial improvement in vegetation.

Under present structures, hill farming, in free market terms, is an uneconomic activity, a large part of its income being in the form of subsidies. Yet the value of hill sheep in providing foundation stock for crossing with lowland stock is considerable, and there is still a deficit of 'sheep meat' in the EEC. Production, which is being increased by changes from the traditional pattern – to more intensive methods, such as with additional winter feed, – is significant in the total agricultural spectrum. Any major changes in the pattern of hill farming would have a serious effect on rural communities. This is particularly important in areas like the Borders where sheep farming has an unbroken tradition back to the twelfth century monks of Melrose, and a way of life that has contributed much to the mainstream of Scottish life. It is also important in the Highlands but over much of this area intensification, such as may be appropriate on the Border hills, is not applicable in the same way. Finding the best ways of integrating sheep farming within broad land-use policies on the poorer land requires determined support through research and development.

Forestry

Scotland has about 950000 hectares of woodlands, 12 per cent of the total land surface (the total area covered in England and Wales is about the same). Conifers occupy about 800000 hectares. Most European countries have between 25 and 30 per cent of their land forested. The most heavily planted areas of Scotland are in Dumfries/Galloway, and Moray/Nairn (16 and 25 per cent respectively).

Forestry had virtually to make a fresh start after the First World War but the pace of development increased markedly after 1945. Much of the planting since the Second World War has been in large blocks of single species trees, sitka spruce, in particular. Government agriculture and forestry policy has pointed the Forestry Commission and private landowners toward the relatively poor quality upland areas, and this has largely decided the type of forestry practised.

Despite the years of expansion, 90 per cent of our timber is still imported but as the new plantations come to maturity it is hoped that this will be reduced, and if a suggested planting programme of about 30000 hectares per year is achieved, eventually about 25 per cent of requirements should be provided. In due course the need for new land for planting will end and a rotation will be established. Softwoods are used for pulpwood, chip and other fabricated board, palletwood and the building industry. There have been predictions that the major supplying countries will not be able to maintain their present level of exports, far less increase them. The timescale for a softwood crop varies from 40 to 70 years with thinnings taken for pulpwood, and other products at about 15 and 30 years.

There is considerable concern about the encroachment of plantations into the remaining wild lands of Scotland. A number of reasons have been given:

(1) Large scale planting is a radical change of land-use with a severe effect on the flora and fauna of the area.

(2) Scotland has areas of unique beauty and interest in the uplands which derive their appeal from the uninterrupted vistas of open country. To some people the introduction of extensive plantations detracts from the scenic quality.

(3) Insensitive siting of plantations and the use of single species has produced a featureless and near sterile landscape.

(4) Ploughing and the cutting of forest roads have caused erosion and problems of water run-off. The planting of conifers on shallow soils has resulted in acidification. Deep ploughing produces root systems on trees that makes them subject to windthrow (breaking out of the soil).

(5) The movement of timber in economic loads is impossible on the Scottish road system.

(6) The use of single species puts the investment at unacceptable risk of destruction, for example, by pine beauty moth or great spruce bark beetle, or of unacceptable methods of controlling them.

(7) Post-war planting has largely been publicly financed, but the last 20 years has seen the development of financial groups attracted by the incentives to make the necessary long-term investments. This tends to remove control of land-use even further from the local community.

(8) There is no planning control over changes from agriculture to forestry. The Forestry Commission administers planting grants through a 'gentleman's agreement' which requires that all major proposals for new planting should be referred to them, and who claim that all community interests are considered before approval is given. This 'agreement' has, however recently been breached on several occasions when the commercial advantages of proceeding in defiance of the Commission's recommendations have exceeded the value of the planting grant.

The following responses have been made:

(1) Much of the upland areas, like all the lowlands, is man-made as a result of the exploitative extraction of timber (without replacement planting) over hundreds of years; and of enclosure, draining, and liming, mainly in the nineteenth century. The question is not whether virgin wilderness should be conserved but whether the *status quo* should be preserved. A policy combining farming and forestry (the norm in most European countries) by the proper siting of plantations could benefit the land and improve the amenities.

(2) Sitka spruce has a much superior yield over all other conifers in exposed upland areas of poor soil. Improvement in amenity can come partly through planting some birch, sycamore, larch and rowan (it has to be realised that this is purely cosmetic and not commercial), but far more importantly by contouring the plantations. For, while modern high tensile fencing must be run in straight lines, the planting within it can be planned to follow the curve of a hill, at the loss of only a small amount of land. Sensitive planting can improve the appearance of bleak moorland.

(3) There is interest in widening the range of species grown, but results with sitka in typical upland conditions are so much better than for any other species that it has no commercial rival. The indigenous conifer, the Scots pine, does not produce comparable yields in these conditions, requiring a drier, less exposed environment with lighter soils, as in the Eastern Highlands. Recent research has, however suggested that improved growth rates can be achieved by using selected mixtures of tree species in spruce plantations.

(4) A plantation can offer a fertile environment for wildlife for at least the first 15 years of its life. Proper scheduling of planting in an area can enhance the prospects of wildlife, especially when associated with sensible farming practices.

(5) There is a far better understanding of acidification, windthrow, water yield and other problems today, and some solutions are already standard practice. Deep ploughing has been substantially reduced and replaced by deep tine ploughing or other methods. Broadleaved trees should be planted along the line of water courses.

There has been much discussion on the use of better class agricultural land for forestry, in particular for the planting of broadleaved trees, but including commercial plantations of softwoods and shelterbelts. This seems a desirable development, especially if it can be integrated with agriculture, although it is difficult to see how the financial problems of a 100/120 year cycle for broadleaved trees can be solved. The quality and yield of timber from the upland areas will tend to be lower than, for example, in Scandinavia where the long-established forests are often associated with deeper soils, and where the exposure to high winds is less; but in a world of increasingly scarce resources the timber requirements of the future are such that a substantial amount of planting must be done in the uplands. The question is not how to stop it, but how it can best be achieved in the interests of the whole community and how to do as little violence to nature as possible.

Deer forests and grouse moors

'Sporting' estates were developed in the last two decades of the nineteenth century, and, while they declined between the Wars, they still represent two thirds of the Highland land area. Ninety per cent of estates rate 'sport' as important, and for one third it is the major activity. In the post-war period, and especially in the last ten years, there have been considerable changes. While many estates are still run for the owners' personal sport and recreation, new commercial managements have developed in different ways the economic exploitation of the resources of the estates. There has been a huge rise in the red deer population since the War. The present total is believed to be about 270000 (this is thought by some to be nearly double the number that the area should carry, however no detailed study appears to have been carried out recently).

Although the number of deer shot has increased by 40 per cent in the last ten years and the market for venison on the Continent, and latterly in the UK, has steadily grown, there are many heavily over-stocked estates where the will or the ability to reduce numbers does not exist, especially in favour of the rehabilitation of the tree forest. During this period the numbers of keepers and estate staff have declined.

Tourism

Since the War, the tourist industry has developed substantially, covering a wide range of activities – from luxury hotels to camping and caravanning. There are considerable implications for land-use and the lives of rural communities, from caravan parks and camp sites to access to hill land, from the letting of cottages and the sale of local produce to litter and vandalism of property and stock. Winter sports have a substantial following and there is controversy over proposed sites for development.

Nature conservation

All these man-centred activities compete for land which includes some of the last genuine wilderness in Europe and areas of great beauty and variety of plant and animal life. The past 30 years have seen nature conservation in the Highlands becoming a land-use in its own right, attracting Government funds for the management of areas primarily for their wildlife by the adaptation of agricultural, forestry and deer management practices (Rum, Cairngorms, Beinn Eighe, Inverpolly). The process is continuing through the development of areas of Special Scientific Interest under the *Wild Life and Countryside Act*. Valuable as this is, it will only be ultimately successful if it can pass its lessons to the whole of our society – that the land may be used without doing irreparable damage to nature, that man can woo the landscape to create an environment where agriculture, forestry and recreation can be carried on without exploitation of the irreplaceable natural resources of the land.

Conclusions

The situation is full of paradoxes. People who deplore 'absentee' landlords and vast estates owned by an individual or family, and who resent the shooting of animals for 'sport', find that some sporting estates can be exemplars of nature conservation where the public is largely excluded and where the only major violence to the environment is where the hillsides have been bulldozed for access by vehicles. Traditional, independent-minded farmers survive on subsidies, with their future hammered out in Brussels, by administrators who have never seen a hill farm. The financial incentives for planting trees are of little advantage to individual farmers, but have attracted investment from distant high rate taxpayers and from pension funds through companies designed to take advantage of the system.

The rural population has gained some advantages from all the developments, but has little fundamental control over its future and in many areas is in steady decline. It must seem to local communities that too many of the decisions that shape their lives are in the hands of frequently absent landlords; a Forestry Commission suffering from savage cuts and heavy governmental pressure; forestry companies remotely controlled and concerned (quite legitimately) with maximum economic exploitation; faceless politicians and bureaucrats in the Community strangled by an unworkable system; tourists who bring all their own supplies with them and spend little in the area; amenity and conservation bodies that seem sometimes to have a remote and rarefied view of life and a willingness to ride roughshod over local interests. Radical changes of land-use in the uplands will take place in the next few years, and it is essential that all the interests in the community should participate in deciding what policies should be adopted.

(c) Wildlife

To many, the word wildlife brings to mind mammals and birds. More thought brings in trees and flowering plants, but perhaps not a recognition of the 2500 species of native higher plants and ferns, 1300 lichens, 900 mosses and liverworts, 70 mammals, reptiles and amphibians, 150 breeding birds and 100 or more regular visitors and over 20000 species of insects and other invertebrates. The reasons for conserving this heritage include scientific, economic and moral components. Most important is the broad aim to prevent any reduction in this variety resulting from man's activities. Active conservation is directed at communities of plants and animals with a view to protecting their habitats. The expectation is that by protecting habitats, the species which depend on them will find the space to live. It is the perception that this variety of habitats in the countryside is threatened which provides much of the impetus for the nature conservation movement. The movement has had mixed success and failure. Some threatened species of plants, birds and animals are now in a healthy state, there is however, a long list of species at risk. But the major concern of nature conservationists has been the loss of natural habitats since 1950 due to changes of land-use.

The movement has developed substantially since the Second World War. It has, in recent years, received more interest from the political parties, while voluntary conservation organisations have grown considerably. The Royal Society for the Protection of Birds, the largest nature conservation body in Europe, has about 400000 members in the UK. It has to be said that the greatest support for nature conservation comes from the urban middle class while in rural areas there is still much scepticism and cynicism as to its value to the community.

Government concern for wildlife was expressed by the

establishment of the Nature Conservancy in 1949; it became the Nature Conservancy Council (NCC) in 1973. Under the Act of 1949 the NCC was given power to establish National Nature Reserves and Sites of Special Scientific Interest by buying, leasing or by entering into management agreements with the landowner. In addition reserves have been developed by other bodies as shown in Table 2:1 in Chapter 2. The major legislation affecting wildlife is now the *Wild Life and Countryside Act* of 1981, which replaced a number of earlier provisions. The Act has two major parts: Part I is concerned with the protection of wild birds, animals and plants, listing protected species and entrusting the NCC with the revision of these lists. However, changes of land-use have led to a rapid and continuing decline in the area and quality of the remaining wildlife habitats since 1950. In an attempt to halt this decline, Part II of the Act developed existing provisions for the establishment of any site of special scientific interest 'by reason of its flora, fauna or geological or physiographical features'. These areas were to be identified by the NCC; the local planning authority, the owner or occupier and the Secretary of State were to be notified. Any alterations of land-use have to be notified to the NCC, but the Council has very limited powers to prevent change. These include compulsory purchase, or the making of compensatory payments to the owner or occupier of the land. This has led to the NCC focusing primarily on the preservation of those habitats which retain their natural structure to the greatest extent.

There are today about 1075 Sites of Special Scientific Interest (SSSIs) in Scotland forming about 7.5 per cent of the land area. The greatest value of the SSSI concept is in the areas where land-use is intensive, where small sites are relatively clearly demarcated and where agricultural or forestry development would be impracticable.

In the upland areas, as the intensity of land-use decreases and the extent of the wildlife habitat is increased, the protection of the SSSI becomes less effective. It might be said that the system works reasonably well in protecting the remaining fragments of habitat in a developed landscape but does little to stem a tide of rapid and radical change of land-use, particularly in upland areas. It is also obvious that concentration on limited areas is a departure from 'an integrated concept of nature conservation' covering the whole land area and can provide a convenient 'let out' for the destruction of natural habitats outside the SSSIs.

However, it is equally clear that SSSIs and nature reserves can never meet all the needs of the rich and varied wildlife listed above. Farmland occupies much of the land surface, and even on the most intensive farms there remain areas presenting opportunities (albeit limited), for wildlife. These opportunities depend not only on the more-or-less degraded fragments of wildlife habitat on the farm, but also on farm management. One aspect of this is certainly the continuing removal of the semi-natural fragments as a result of changing farming practice, but the second is the extent to which operations on the farmed land are compatible with the wild species making use of that ground.

There are strong arguments about the principle of payments for conservation. On the one side, it is suggested that the idea of positive conservation as a source of income for upland farmers is desirable and might well be extended (obviously as part of an overall review of grants and subsidies); on the other side, the comparison with planning regulations for listed buildings is made and it has been suggested that fictional development proposals might well be introduced for the sole purpose of attracting compensation.

Most cases of major change of land-use in Scotland

involve the planting of conifers, often of a single species in very large areas, on upland sites. Control of the areas has been exercised by a 'gentleman's agreement', by which the Forestry Commission approves the planting proposals and pays the planting grant. DAFS (Department of Agriculture and Fisheries, Scotland) may refuse permission for land to be transferred out of agricultural use, in which case no planting grant is paid; but nothing can stop the owner of the land from going ahead with planting and still receiving the tax concessions. The establishment of SSSIs proves a weak defence because of their limited area and the limited power of the NCC. The absence of any control over land planning is a major problem for nature conservation.

(d) The Rural Community

It has been estimated that only 20 per cent of the population lives on 85 per cent of the land area which can be regarded as rural, yet Scotland's population was predominantly rural until the middle of the nineteenth century. Until the late eighteenth century the habitable rural areas, that is the glens, straths, coastal fringes and islands, were much more densely populated, despite high mortality, poor diet, housing and health care. The radical change of land-use to sheep farming had, as one of its consequences, a drastic reduction in the rural population, while the urban concentration of the central belt developed rapidly. Since then the rural population of Scotland has been in decline and the urban population has been increasingly alienated from the countryside. The second radical change was the rise of the sporting estates late in the nineteenth century and this also had important human consequences. This is not the place to discuss the history and morality of the Clearances, but it has to be said that those who have had control over the use of land in the past 200 years have had an important influence on the distribution, employment and lifestyle of a significant proportion of Scotland's population. The history of the period continues to have a profound effect on the culture and the attitudes of the Highland population.

This century has seen a steady reduction in the rural population, caused mainly by a decline in employment in the primary sector – agriculture. Between 1951 and 1979 the number of agricultural workers declined from 50000 to 35000. Despite the increase in forestry, the number directly employed is only about 7000. As peaks of employment are for planting and felling, the use of contractors is common, often from outside the area of work. Increasingly, forestry workers live in towns and travel to work. Since the 1950s, through increased leisure time and disposable income, there has been a rapid increase of rural recreation and, more recently, signs of increased interest in rural living.

In the years of full employment in the industrial areas, those rural workers who lost their jobs had every incentive to move to the towns, which also had social attractions. After some years of high unemployment the temptations of urban living are much reduced. The loss of population is, however, both a cause and a consequence of changes in the provision of rural services: the primary school and the Post Office may close, the bus services decline and the provision of health services diminish. The desire for higher education has for decades been one of the strongest pressures to move, especially on the young and able, and the lack of sufficient opportunities in the rural areas for the highly qualified has ensured that many never return.

It is essential to the well being of the whole country that there should be a reasonably prosperous rural community and this too has important implications for responsible land-use. Such prosperity depends on sustainable primary employment, that is, in agriculture and, to a lesser extent in forestry, but even if changes in systems were introduced the effect on employment would probably not be dramatic. Proposals for new structures of ownership or new farming systems require much more research and experiment. Perhaps the best that can be hoped for is that the decline can be arrested. The employment possibilities for tourism and for recreation are more promising. The seasonal nature of much of this employment results in multi-employment becoming a normal pattern, but it also provides secondary income for established families. Rural communities often have an ambivalent attitude to the influx of visitors, whether winter sports enthusiasts, summer holidaymakers, day trippers or second homers. Additional trade to shops, garages and hotels is balanced by choked road systems and farm damage. The effect on the local housing market of the increasing numbers of second and retiral homes may be considerable, but on the other hand many houses have been rescued from becoming derelict.

Attempts to establish major new industries in the rural area have largely been unsuccessful. North Sea fabrication yards, probably with a limited future, have provided employment though much of the workforce has come from outside the area and the yards have brought with them social and environmental problems. The communities concerned will have to measure the costs and benefits to them, if, as seems likely, nuclear or military installations are sited in the remote areas. They may, however, not be the final arbiters.

While agriculture must remain the basic economic activity, future growth in the rural community appears to depend on a relatively affluent, mobile and independent population choosing to live in the countryside, either as commuters with an improved road system, or engaged in some form of employment which information technology allows to be operated anywhere. Some possibilities do exist for the establishment of small scale industry. There are likely to be increases in the numbers choosing what they consider to be a traditional way of life, for example, small-holding or craft work. Some small, but encouraging, signs of a revitalisation in existing rural populations have been evident in the emergence of community co-operatives, particularly in crofting areas. A wide range of activities (such as fish-farming, horticulture, building and agricultural supplies, cafés and mobile shops, weaving, knitwear, peat-cutting), are based on the concept of using local resources, both human and natural, to provide the goods and services the community actually needs. They indicate the possibilities for a more diverse, and thus more stable, local economy. Furthermore, they have the effect of increasing self-confidence within a community who see that they themselves can initiate and control efforts to stem the loss of population and amenities from their area, and so create a more positive atmosphere for the generation of a variety of local economic enterprises alongside the traditional farming base.

The growth in the number of people choosing the rural areas for retirement is a matter for concern. New residents may bring alien and contradictory values and demands. They may put more stress on existing land-uses and require more public access to the countryside. They may be vociferous in objecting to some rural working practices or institutions, to afforestation or to housing development. Despite the wide differences of experience and outlook of the modern rural population, it is highly desirable that they should be consulted before policies involving major changes in land-use are agreed. Obviously some changes have a more immediate impact, such as new road systems or the introduction of industry, but changes in agriculture and forestry policies can also affect the quality of life of a community.

(e) The relationship of the Urban Community to the Land

More than 80 per cent of Scotland's population lives in urban areas, mainly in the Central Lowlands. The industrial towns of west and central Scotland developed in a remarkably short time when the population of the north flocked, or was driven, to become, with the immigrant Irish, the labour force for the Industrial Revolution. Basic needs of food, warmth and shelter were all that were initially provided; overcrowding, pollution and disease were all accepted. The alienation of town from country had begun. Yet concern for the urban environment started in the 1850s with the establishment of the great Glasgow parks. Towards the end of the century prophetic figures such as Ebenezer Howard and Patrick Geddes raised questions and proposed solutions to the environmental problems of industrial towns. Their influence has been profound although many of the lessons they and their disciples taught have still to be completely absorbed. While the effects of surroundings on the human organism are better understood today, they have still received remarkably little attention. Progress has been made on slum clearance and improvement of housing standards (although sometimes at a terrible social cost and sometimes by exchanging one problem for another), but only relatively recently has full recognition been given to the effects of immediate surroundings on mental health.

This aspect of human welfare involves not only the improvement of the built environment, the re-instatement of the inner city, the regeneration of derelict industrial land and the provision of 'oases' in the concrete jungle in the form of parks and gardens (bringing the country into the city), but also the provision of access to the real countryside. The latter is desirable for physical health alone, considering the levels of pollution and reduction of sunshine even in the cleanest cities, but for the less readily measured but equally important attribute of mental health it is well-nigh essential. Because the human species evolved in an environment of hills and plains, forests and steppes, trees, plants and animals, even civilised man seems to need recourse to some of the features in which his special characteristics emerged. While cities or some parts of them, may provide a satisfying environment, this is not so for the great majority of city dwellers who are therefore to a greater or lesser degree 'deprived' if, for whatever reasons, they cannot have access to the country. Many may not recognise a lack, but this is not to deny its existence.

The mobile middle classes have always believed in the importance of access to the countryside. However, it is true to say that while, on the one hand, the split between town and country has been greater in Scotland than in England (in Scotland, there is little of the English nostalgia for village life); on the other hand, in many ways stronger links are retained by the whole Scottish community, partly for reasons of geography (it is far easier to have access to the hills), partly through a continuing interest in agriculture (as shown by the amount of space devoted to it in the national press), partly because of a nostalgia for a 'golden' past and a romantic attachment to the landscape.

There is a fundamental need for access to the countryside and for facilities for recreation there. This is recognised by society by the allocation of public funds to bodies such as the Countryside Commission for Scotland, which is charged with the responsibility to help to improve the facilities for people's enjoyment of the countryside, and to safeguard its beauty for their enjoyment now and in the future.

This approach has a number of important implications.

For example, it follows that it is appropriate for towns-people to have some say in what goes on in the country-side, for this affects the capacity of the country to satisfy their legitimate needs for recreation. They will expect to be able to travel to the country and move about in it with reasonable freedom, and to indulge in sports such as walking, riding, skiing, boating and so on. In looking for this degree of accommodation they are, in fact, merely acting as members of 'the public', and not specifically as townspeople; for many members of rural communities have the same concerns.

In urging a more positive relationship between the urban population and the countryside, it is essential to maintain a balanced view. Clearly, the needs and wishes of those who live in towns cannot be allowed to inhibit all change in the countryside merely to satisfy a sentimental attachment to things as they are. Nor should 'the public' expect unrestricted access at all times to places where others gain their living, or where the conservation of nature requires some control. No one can expect co-operation unless they take the trouble to understand the principles upon which the countryside works, whether it is 'wilderness' or productive. A vital component of im-proved use of the countryside by townspeople, therefore, is adequate education and interpretation, which is another extremely important aspect of the work of con-servation bodies, including the Countryside Commission. Without it, the essential understanding between urban and rural communities cannot be fostered. It needs to embrace not only the functioning of the natural world of the countryside, but also farming, forestry and other economic activities. The popularity and success of 'Family days on the farm' gives some indication of the value of this kind of education.

Increasing use of the countryside for recreation has its attendant problems, even when visitors are as well-informed as possible. The sheer pressure of many visitors and their cars arriving at popular locations is often sufficient to cause disruption of vegetation, soil erosion and loss of the very resource they have come to enjoy. Their numbers may disturb the animals or birds on which estates or farms depend for their economic viability, or the wellbeing of the wild animals or plants. If townspeople expect to have a share of influence on what happens in the country, they must equally accept restrictions, to make their presence compatible with the continued functioning of the rural economy. This requires effective management, an art still in its infancy in this country, and which involves the identification of relatively robust localities capable of accepting large numbers of visitors, the ability to judge when these numbers have reached the limits which the area can accommodate, and arrangements to divert people to other sites at peak times. Further studies are also needed on the best ways to rehabilitate damaged vegetation, over-used paths and so on. However, once the mechanisms for accepting and integrating people into chosen parts of the countryside are better developed, both urban and rural dwellers should stand to gain and greater harmony should develop. At the same time it should be possible, without interfering with proper rural land-use, to safeguard appropriate 'wilderness' areas for the minority to whom this has a very special appeal and to preserve the unique characteristics of the plants and animals of these areas for the future.

Among active outdoor leisure pursuits of Scots people, walking is the single most popular activity and more than a third of the population is said to go for at least one walk of over two miles each year. The majority of tourists and residents make quite modest requirements on the countryside. Walks tend to be close to towns, hence the importance of parks in the areas in and around industrial towns.

A substantial and growing minority of walkers and climbers make longer excursions and can have a significant effect on the environment and impact on the rural population. Particularly serious local effects are felt in popular areas like the Cairngorms and Ben Nevis, while the development of skiing on Cairn Gorm, in Glencoe, Glenshee and the Lecht has obvious environmental consequences.

In 1974 the Countryside Commission published a report proposing a national system of parks. Urban parks are the mainly long established parks in our towns and cities. Their link with other park provisions was seen to be increasingly important for the future. Country parks, designated and managed by district or regional authorities are relatively small (between 10 and 400 hectares) with fairly intensive use. There are more than 20 such parks in Scotland, all situated within easy reach of the urban areas. The idea of much larger Regional Parks was pioneered by Renfrew County Council, now part of Strathclyde Region, in the Clyde-Muirshiel Regional Park, which extends over 12000 hectares and within which recreation is the dominant use in parts only. These areas are linked together by footpaths, thus reducing the pressure on neighbouring farming and forestry lands. A second Regional park has been proposed for the Pentland Hills. Finally, the Commission suggested a category of special parks, areas already under substantial recreational pressure and having characteristics which give them a national rather than a regional or local significance. Such characteristics would justify some national control and the provision of financial support.

The Countryside Commission proposed that separate authorities should be set up for each park, with two-thirds of the members coming from local authorities and one-third from central government, the latter to represent the scenic, recreational, scientific and other aspects.

This idea has not found universal support; however, the plan for Loch Lomond is significant. The other areas which the Commission considered as important and obvious were the Cairngorms and the Glencoe/Ben Nevis complex.

Beyond the park system and the needs of urban recreation, there is a need to conserve the scenic resources of the country. Forty such areas have been identified in the first overall assessment of Scottish scenery. They total over a million hectares, 12.83 per cent of the land. Within them there are certain planning restrictions and the Commission can negotiate management agreements with landowners in the interest of scenic conservation. The report does not, of course, deal with the overall question of land-use or with the future of the wild land areas, but provides a useful framework for developing a sensible relationship between the urban communities and the land.

(f) Pollution

Environmental pollution is not new, but in recent years a new awareness of its significance to both man and nature has developed. In this country we have escaped some of the more devastating effects, thanks largely to our control arrangements; however there is no room for complacency.

Pollution can be considered under four heads, marine, atmosphere, land, and fresh waters and river estuaries, each interrelated and affecting the others.

Two great 'global commons' – the oceans and the atmosphere – are important in the dispersal of many pollutants. These include radioactive substances which, along with marine pollution, are outside the scope of this account. Marine pollution which covers oil spillage, waste dumping and discharges from land sources is touched upon, but only in so far as pollutant discharges to fresh waters are discussed.

Atmospheric pollution – changes in perspective

Concern about the effects of severely polluted air on city dwellers goes back many centuries. From the early days of coal-burning, coal smoke and associated gases such as sulphur dioxide (SO_2) have caused problems. However, it took the notorious London smog in December 1952 (which in three days caused about 4000 deaths, mostly from respiratory disorders) to produce the political will to control the problem. Four years later the *Clean Air Act 1956* was passed.

The new measures directly reduced smoke emissions. Indirectly, they also decreased 'low level' emissions of SO_2 as the domestic use of coal diminished, and a larger proportion of the gases were emitted through tall chimneys at power stations. This legislation led to a growing interest in questions of human health. With the increasing number and amounts of chemicals released into the environment since that time, this trend has been further reinforced. Moreover, with the realisation that damaging pollutants, including substances that form secondary pollutants, can be carried in air masses for hundreds of kilometres, air pollution has come to the forefront as a political and international issue.

A change has also taken place in understanding how air pollutants affect plants and animals. From early in the last century pollution damage to plants has been noted in many countries, for example, where severe fumigation from industrial sources has affected trees locally. It is now realised that comparatively modest concentrations of pollutants can be harmful. It has also been recognised that damaging effects on plants are not necessarily accompanied by visual blemishes and that certain pollutants, when present in mixtures, can be injurious at concentrations once thought to be unimportant.

Acid rain – an international problem

At the United Nations Conference on the Human Environment, held in Stockholm in 1972, Sweden claimed that increasing sulphur emissions to the atmosphere had increased the acidity of rain causing an increase in the deposition of excess acid in southern Sweden and Norway, and that this was responsible for killing fish in rivers and lakes. Thousands of lakes are now affected and in many, fish stocks have been completely destroyed.

After emission from a chimney SO_2 gas is deposited at ground level on surfaces such as buildings, soils or plant leaves. This so-called dry deposition can injure plants. The sulphur remaining in the atmosphere may be transported a long way as the SO_2 is gradually oxidised to sulphuric acid. When rain falls, polluted raindrops deposit their contents; so-called wet deposition. Thus British sources contribute to acidity deposited in Norway and Sweden.

In rain falling over Scotland about 70 per cent of the acidity occurs as sulphuric acid and 30 per cent as nitric acid originating from oxides of nitrogen. The total deposition at a particular place is made up of wet deposition arriving as rain or mist, along with the acidity generated when the acid-forming gases (SO_2 and nitrogen dioxide) are deposited by dry deposition. The term 'acid rain' is sometimes used to describe this total acidity deposited by wet and dry processes.

Damage to lakes and watercourses is now found in many places in Europe, Canada, and the USA and, in 1983, acidification was detected in Galloway. Acidification of Loch Grannoch and Round Loch of Glenhead had apparently taken place during the late nineteenth and twentieth centuries, and the evidence pointed to the atmospheric origin of the increased acidity. The Galloway lochs overlying granitic rocks are particularly susceptible, but other areas of Scotland where geological conditions may predispose the land to acidification lie north of the Highland line.

As well as affecting fresh waters and the plants and animals dependent on them acid rain (or mist) can have adverse effects on plants including crops and trees. The circumstances in which this may occur under Scottish conditions is yet to be determined.

Other airborne pollutants

Sulphur dioxide, along with smoke, was an important form of air pollution in the Central Belt in the first half of this century. Effects today of the gaseous pollutants SO_2 and oxides of nitrogen on economically important trees and crops are likely to be small. Hydrocarbons are emitted from the internal combustion engine and from various industrial sources such as the petrochemical complex at Grangemouth and the new development at Mossmorran in Fife. Pollutant ozone is generated by light-triggered reactions in air containing unburnt hydrocarbons and oxides of nitrogen, both of which, along with the ozone produced, can injure plants.

The so-called heavy metals such as lead and cadmium can be hazardous to people and wildlife. They accumulate in urban and roadside soils. The nature of wider dispersion is uncertain but in some parts of the world atmospherically dispersed heavy metals are implicated in damage to forests. Damage to plants and animals by fluorine, a pollutant in a different category, is essentially a local problem. In the 1940s fluoride injury to livestock and tree foliage occurred in a small area near the Fort William smelter. Effects on animals and plants have also been noticed elsewhere.

Two problems should be noted here, in the Bonnybridge/Denny area, where waste incineration has been suspected of being implicated in the occurrence of human and animal disorders, and in Armadale where the incidence of human respiratory cancer is reported to be high.

Pollution of land and freshwaters – improving conditions of industrial pollution

The whole of the earth's surface is a catchment area, receiving pollutants deposited from the atmosphere. These augment those discharged into freshwaters from urban sources and from agriculture.

The state of water-courses in the industrial parts of Scotland in the last century can be gauged from a Royal Commission Report of 1872, '...the Dighty, Lothian Esk and Almond, the Gala and Kilmarnock water, the Kelvin and the Cart are hardly equalled anywhere for filthiness; and the Clyde is beautiful or disgusting according as it is taken in the upper or lower section of its course'.

It was only in the 1950s that a really effective system of river pollution administration and control was established when nine river purification boards were set up. Further legislation (including the *Control of Pollution Act 1974*) extended control by river purification authorities. All this, together with the *European Community Environmental Directives,* provides an administrative framework for further progress to be made in pollution control. Increasingly, River Boards' surveillance work includes such issues as pesticide residues, trace metals and acidification in upland streams. Although both sewage and trade effluents still pollute some Scottish rivers, their condition has clearly been revolutionised since the 1872 Report. In their *Annual Report* the Clyde River Purification Board (1984) noted the return of salmon in 1983 after an absence of 120 years.

Pollution from agriculture

Discharges from agricultural land include nitrates, animal wastes, silage effluent and pesticide residues. New legislation, in the form of the *Food and Environment Protection Act 1985,* introduces comprehensive measures concerning food contamination and the use of pesticides. Large concentrations of nitrates in streams and groundwater used for human consumption can be a threat to health. The problem is less severe than in some parts of Britain as only 10 per cent of water supplies are drawn from the lower reaches of rivers and 3 per cent from groundwater. Nitrates from land drainage or sewage effluent can also cause eutrophication – nutrient enrichment – of surface waters. This can lead to excessive growth of algae which presents problems both in water supply and wildlife conservation. In the disposal of animal wastes care is needed to prevent the contamination of water-courses with wastes that spread disease, or with silage effluent that can kill fish and other aquatic life. Many problems of contamination can be overcome by good farming practice, but modern techniques of intensive animal management create disposal problems that have yet to be satisfactorily resolved.

The agrochemical industry since the Second World War has produced successive generations of organic compounds for many uses in the control of pests, diseases and growth regulation in crops. The introduction of these chemicals has enabled highly intensive farming systems to evolve, but not without adverse environmental effects such as resulted from the use of persistent organo-chlorine insecticides (DDT, aldrin and dieldrin for example). Since 1962 successive Government restrictions have curtailed the use of these polluting compounds. Nevertheless, reports have shown that some use continued into the 1980s. Unfortunately, there is a tendency not only for the long-lived derivitives of DDT to build up in river estuaries, but Polychlorinated biphenyls (PCBs) and heavy metals show a similar tendency.

The Royal Commission on Environmental Pollution in their *Seventh Report 1979* discussed problems in the use of chemicals in modern agricultural and forestry practice. They stressed the need for minimal use, bearing in mind possible long-term effects on people. With regard to ecological effects it is hardly practicable to achieve a foolproof basis for prediction.

Air pollution and climatic change

Several gases, including carbon dioxide and nitrous oxide, when they accumulate, have the capacity, to change the heat balance of the earth and increase the temperature; the so-called greenhouse effect. Both these gases are generated on a global scale. Carbon dioxide, is released to the atmosphere when fossil fuels are burnt and by deforestation. The concentration of carbon dioxide has already increased by 14 per cent since the industrial era began and during the next century, concentrations are expected to reach levels previously unknown. The precise effects on our climate are still uncertain but we face the expectation that changed conditions will affect agriculture, forestry and wildlife. This prospect is within the time span of a single rotation of Sitka spruce.

Comment

To sum up, polluting activities can be conveniently distinguished into three overlapping categories: local or catchment scale effects; more widespread regional effects; and those on a global scale. Notwithstanding the great strides that have been made with many problems in the first category, we cannot be satisfied with the condition of some waterways or with circumstances noted in the Central Belt. The latter in particular illustrates how much there is still to learn about how early-warning signals should be evaluated. On the regional scale, Scotland contributes to the acidity of rain falling over western and northwest Europe. Only concerted international action can resolve this issue. It is not surprising that many countries affected have expressed profound disappointment that Britain has so far refused to sign the binding protocol, as others have done, to reduce SO_2 emissions by at least 30 per cent by 1993.

The prospect of climatic change illustrates the sheer scale and scope of pollution effects. Manufacturing industry, fuel use and certain agricultural practices all over the world – along with the fate of the natural forests in tropical countries – all affect the processes in the atmospheric global common that will influence the world's climatic patterns. Intractible though it may seem to be on this scale, the problem is not just symbolic, it is a real pollution issue that we can expect to influence our domestic policies and our international obligations: it cannot be ignored.

In all aspects of pollution, responsibility here in Scotland requires that we scrutinise not just our current practices, but the fundamental principles on which our industrialised society operates; what we produce, how we produce it, where we do so, and the consequences of our actions. This applies to agriculture and forestry also. Moreover there are grounds for concern that there is insufficient understanding that impacts of polluting substances cannot be properly identified or evaluated simply by seeking evidence of gross and obvious effects, whether in terms of human health, wildlife, crop or timber production.

Finally, in trying to establish a harmonious relationship with our environment – the only basis on which a stable order can be built – we must recognise that delicate biological balances are involved; disturbance or disruption in subtle ways may take a long time to show and, when they do, effects may be expressed in unexpected forms. Economic activity is often responsible for generating its own constraints or increasing, if not its costs, then frequently the costs or penalties which others must bear, whether now or in the future. Once this principle is fully grasped the way is open for real advances to be made in controlling pollution of all kinds.

(g) Economics

Crisis in agriculture

The economic influences which have shaped the policy decisions of farmers, foresters and others involved in land-use over the past ten years are made up of a confused mixture of the pressures of the consumer market, the development of new techniques, the Common Agricultural Policy and UK taxation policy. The policies that have been followed are in essence the same as those that have applied in other industries – increased mechanisation with consequent reduction in labour, specialisation, increased uniformity of products, larger scale, the elimination of the craft element in favour of production-line systems and a large increase in energy and materials consumption. Since Britain's entry into the EEC the major economic force that shapes agriculture is the Common Agricultural Policy; the Policy is in serious trouble and it is clear that a substantial reappraisal is required.

The *Treaty of Rome* of 1957 set up the European Community as a Customs Union of six states, but having as its long-term aim the political unity of Europe. The Common Agricultural Policy was the only form of positive integration envisaged by the Treaty. Its stated aims were:

(1) to increase agricultural productivity by promoting

technical progress and the best uses of the resources of land and labour;
(2) to ensure a fair standard of living for the agricultural community;
(3) to stabilise markets;
(4) to assure availability of supplies;
(5) to ensure a reasonable price for consumers.

The cost of implementing it has placed a heavy financial burden on the Community; in 1984 two-thirds of the budget went to agriculture. The CAP has been criticised for establishing prices above world market levels within the market, of creating surpluses of various commodities and of distorting world trade by putting these heavily subsidised stocks on the market.

It should be noted that despite a number of contradictory intentions the CAP has had considerable success; Europe is self-sufficient in most basic foodstuffs, and the agricultural community, although smaller, is reasonably prosperous. The original intentions of the Six were significantly different from those of Britain, in particular because the much higher number of people employed on the land, especially in Italy and France (but also in Germany and even in the Netherlands) was an important political factor. Despite the need to support a large number of very small farms, especially in southern Europe, it can be said that broadly the CAP has favoured large scale highly mechanised and intensive farming, and has encouraged productivity above all else.

In the UK, although the number of people involved in agriculture is relatively small, in Scotland about 35000, agriculture is still a major employer and when the occupations directly related to agriculture are added, the number more than doubles. Substantial activity is also generated in the transport and distribution sectors. Obviously its importance as an employer and a provider of employment is very great in the rural areas.

Proposals for change

Despite the unacceptably high cost of the CAP, there has been a catastrophic slump in Scotland's farm incomes in the 1980s, which in real terms are far below the levels of the 1970s. Scottish farm income is reported to have dropped by 75 per cent in 1985, and though the atrocious weather has been a major reason, these conditions hide a continuing downward trend. This economic crisis is of great importance to the whole community and the development of sensible long-term policies for agriculture is a major political question.

Suggestions for policy direction to curb the rising cost to the Community have been many and varied. Most of them propose variations of the present CAP support system and have included reductions in support prices, the introduction of quotas for cereals, a 'set aside' policy which involves payment to farmers for leaving land fallow, taxes on inputs (such as fertilisers) or deficiency payments. There are numerous other suggestions.

Some economists and politicians have suggested abandoning all agricultural support and the restoration of a free market. They claim that this would not only produce lower prices for the consumer through the survival of the fittest, but would also result in more conservation of the countryside as marginal farms went out of business. The probable effects of such a policy would be the concentration of agriculture in large, heavily mechanised units operating highly intensive systems situated geographically close to centres of population. Small farms and upland farms in general would tend to disappear in large numbers, with serious consequences for rural communities. Rather than improving conservation it would seem likely to produce rural decay and dereliction.

This is an extreme situation, but severe price reductions within the present framework would tend to produce the same type of result, if in lesser degree. The first farmers to go out of business would probably be those with large scale borrowings, by no means only the inefficient, but often those engaged in improvements, or young farmers setting up in business. Recent forecasts estimate that in ten years 1.3 million hectares of arable land in the UK could be seeking alternative use and that this figure could nearly double in the following five years. The most vulnerable lands are the marginal arable areas, but upland farms, although protected by EEC subsidies may find increased competition as low ground farmers turn to beef production.

Many in the agricultural community believe that a resonable *modus vivendi* can be found. They consider that a policy based on the present systems of farming with such diversification as seems possible, with restrictions on production but with a protected market is the best hope for a viable future. This should be combined with support for marginal areas through the development of other types of land-use – forestry, country parks or wildlife reserves.

The proposals that conservation should be regarded as a commercial activity and that some part of government resources should be diverted to make suitable payments, are important, as are in a minor way, subsidiary suggestions of grants, for example for the repair of dykes and the replacement of hedges. Much more important is the development of a positive policy of integrating farming and forestry, especially if the layout of new plantations is designed in the interests of the land in terms of shelter and of the total environment. But all these measures, added to the vigorous efforts to find new crops or to develop part-time occupations, are likely only to temper the cold wind of lower support prices or other measures.

Others hold strongly the opinion that, as the era when

the search for increased productivity governed all other considerations has ended, this should be marked, not by a battening down of the hatches till the storm blows over, but by a re-examination of the basis of modern farming methods. They suggest that rather than restricting excessive production by reduced support or quota schemes the same result could well be obtained by turning to farming systems which use lower purchased inputs and which would offer ecological benefits. In addition this could avoid some of the social costs of a rapid decline of the farming community.

Challenging market realities with an ethic of stewardship concerned both with the human community and with the long-term health of the land and its natural inhabitants does not require a change in the order of our social priorities. It does, however, demand that these priorities take precedence over market forces, which in any case are not free but politically contrived, and which dictate the technologies which producers operate. The market mechanism has to become the servant, not the master. This implies continuing regulation of that mechanism but with a changed emphasis. A solution to the EEC agricultural policy crisis is not to be sought in the 'free market', but in a positive vision of the kind of farming and use of rural resources which government should seek to promote through a combination of inducements and penalties. The importance of environmental objectives has found increasing recognition in official EEC statements relating to agricultural policy, but an articulate constituency must continue to be built in Scotland and in other European countries. Without a substantial body of opinion concerned with long-term policies and responsible land-use, EEC policy reform will continue to result in measures which are conceived in response to an imminent financial crisis but which fail to address the long-term questions of future rural resource use.

The consumer

The attitudes of consumers towards agricultural produce are changing at a pace that has increased rapidly in the past five years. There are a number of reasons; firstly, there is a greater interest in physical health and well-being, demonstrated in worry about the causes of heart disease, obesity, cancer and other diet-linked disorders. Concern for animal welfare and a revulsion against the concept of intensively farmed hens, pigs and other animals has brought a remarkable increase in vegetarianism, while anxiety about the effects of chemicals, both during the growing and in the preparation for market of various commodities, has produced a demand for organically grown produce. Behind all these concerns lies a deep unease about the effect of modern farming methods on the landscape, and on their long-term viability.

It is argued that some of the new attitudes are not based on proper research and owe more to emotion than to reason. Be that as it may, the change in attitudes is striking, but it by no means covers the whole community and still leaves Scotland with the worst diet, the highest incidence of heart disease and the worst teeth in Europe. The idea that the health of a largely urban community, the economic wellbeing of the agricultural community and the responsible use of land might be considered together might seem a novel one. Yet most of the innovations that cause concern were introduced as part of the drive to increased productivity. If productivity is no longer the first priority, then the question of costs may have to be assessed over a wider spectrum. For, example, better standards of nutrition have economic benefits as well as improving the quality of life. Changes of attitude and of practice tend to be slow and major changes in agricultural practice involve economic dislocation and therefore need transitional support. Some changes take longer to introduce than others. For example, a farmer wishing to convert to organic methods will have to go through a conversion period before he can satisfy the requirements of the Organic Standards Committee. This may involve a grass crop in an arable rotation, or 'dedicating' small acreages to organic husbandry before committing the whole farm to such a system. Again, the time taken to produce a leaner type of beef animal is much longer than it takes to alter the method and composition of crop spraying.

The policy decisions being made now will have enduring consequences and should be governed less by the immediate exigencies of the EEC budget crisis but more by a clear perception of the kind of future towards which we are trying to work. This perception should include not only the economic health of the farming industry, the rural community and the long-term aims of responsible land-use, but also the changing needs of society.

5. CASE STUDIES

(b) *Knoydart and the future of the wild lands*

Knoydart is a peninsula of 80 square miles, with 39 miles of coastline. Access is by sea, by helicopter, or by a walk of 15 miles over a 2000-foot pass. It has had a chequered history. After a series of emigrations and evictions in the eighteenth century; 600 people were cleared, mainly forcibly, and transported to Canada in the middle of the nineteenth century, so that the land could be sold for sheep farming. Later, deer-stalking became the principal interest. After the Second World War six men made a 'land raid' and tried to establish rights to crofting, but they were defeated in the courts. From 1973 a new owner attempted to develop the estate creatively, establishing a fish farm, some forestry and a hydro-electric scheme. The population increased from 50 to 80. The financial burden became too heavy and in 1981 the estate was put on the market in the hope that a new owner could be found who would preserve the area.

The National Trust for Scotland had an obvious interest, but had other heavy financial commitments, and regarded the ongoing annual cost of operating the estate, estimated as between £50000 and £100000 per annum, as an impossible burden. Men and women with the varied skills required for the proper management of such a diverse area were also hard to find. The estate remained on the market for more than a year until, in November 1982, the Ministry of Defence showed an interest – as a military range for coastal landings, rifle and mortar training. There was some support for this by Members of Parliament and Regional Councillors as it promised some local employment; but not among the locals, a large

majority of whom strongly opposed the idea. Conservation bodies were, however, even more strongly opposed.
Attempts were made by some organisations to find a way
of purchasing and operating the estate in order to preserve it. The National Heritage Memorial Trust stated
that a grant to purchase might be made, but only if an
established body such as the National Trust took responsibility for managing it. Joint meetings were held between
the Trust, local authorities, the Nature Conservancy
Council and the Countryside Commission for Scotland.
Highland political opinion ranged from suggestions that
the area could be opened up, with road access and the
re-instatement of the pre-Clearances population, to resistance to anything other than private ownership. The
need to develop a long-term strategy to care for the land
in the interest of the whole community is often hindered
by an attachment to romantic and highly impractical
idealism on the one hand and unthinking dogmatism on
the other. At the beginning of 1983 the MOD withdrew.
In April, despite careful reconsideration and discussion
with all the official bodies and with the conservation
organisations, the National Trust for Scotland eventually
confirmed its inability to accept such a heavy long-term
responsibility and also withdrew.

Eventually, in August 1984, the estate was sold to a
private individual. The policies of the new owner are not
the consideration of this case study. Rather, the question
is whether lessons can be learned from the earlier events,
that might help to develop long-term policies to preserve
Scotland's truly wild lands such as Knoydart and other
mountainous country of like grandeur. There are still a
number of large areas of Scotland which have similar
characteristics to Knoydart – of remoteness, of a relatively unspoiled environment, without or with little,
human habitation, of great natural beauty and of great
scenic and historic interest. Such areas may contain sites

of special scientific interest (SSSI's) designated by the NCC or lie within a National Scenic Area (NSA). Knoydart has SSSI's and lies within an NSA, but further provision to ensure the integrity of such areas is required in the interest of the whole community. Instead of last minute attempts by various interested bodies to develop a defensive strategy when some unacceptable development seems to be imminent, these areas should rank as high in our list of national treasures as do our Adam buildings or the Burrell Collection and a positive national policy for their future should be outlined and implemented by Government in the interest of the whole nation.

There is some evidence that financial pressures are already making it impossible for many large estates to be managed as the more enlightened owners would wish. Far too large stocks of red deer are being carried to boost stalking income, and they cause over-grazing, erosion and damage to woodlands and agricultural land. Large estates are being broken up into smaller units which in some cases is to be welcomed, but not where it is environmentally desirable that the area should be managed as a single unit. Huge areas may only employ a single individual so that all the many essential small jobs necessary for good estate-management may be neglected. Alternatively, ownership may fall to exceptionally wealthy absentee lairds, some to foreigners with no roots in the Highlands and others to faceless syndicates, none of whom possess the altruism necessary to secure the future of such valuable Scottish heritage land.

The interests of the MOD should not be ignored. It is obviously essential that suitable training areas should be available. This area had many advantages – remoteness, a varied terrain, a long and relatively sheltered coastline. These considerations have to be set against the serene qualities of the area and the strong body of public opinion which says that it is desirable to preserve in perpetuity an area like Knoydart in its present form. Conservationists might consider that they have a duty to identify areas of Scotland which are suitable for training without such serious ecological consequences.

The balance between preserving land by discouraging access to it and of encouraging the community (especially the urban community), to share its beauty, is a delicate one. One can discount extremists who would like to exclude everyone, except of course themselves, from the hills. However many moderates are critical of damage caused by over-use. It may be that areas should be established with some agreed overall policy of land-use to encourage a viable and healthy local community based on a mix of agriculture, forestry, deer management and fisheries and yet have plenty to offer in tourism and recreation without overbearing restrictions on access. Such areas would help visitors to understand the relationship between man and the environment in the setting of wild country. It is not rational that British people who are financially and morally responsible for the land should be excluded from most of it. The remoteness, the essentially limited facilities, the sheer effort of getting there, will, through human frailty, exclude the majority. However, large-scale tourist operations have to be looked at with scepticism.

Although ten national parks were established in England in 1949, they were not intended, as in the USA or other countries, to be management systems for wild land. They are areas of natural beauty where opportunities exist for open-air recreation, and they are maintained for that purpose. Recreational use and public access is regulated with consideration for existing systems of agriculture, forestry and other economic and social uses of the land, which largely remain in private ownership. Despite the recommendation of the Ramsay Committee in 1945, which advocated the establishment of National

Parks in Scotland, no action was taken. Much less imaginatively, areas which had been identified as potential National Parks were designated as National Park Direction Areas, for which the Secretary of State was empowered to determine the outcome of planning applications. Events in Knoydart, the Cairngorms and Loch Lomond point to this arrangement being inadequate in providing for the future of such important areas.

There have been suggestions that the establishment of Scottish National Parks should be re-considered with the conservation of the remaining 'wild land' areas of Scotland as its primary objective. There are obviously different structures possible for such parks; it is sufficient to say here that their primary purpose should be to sustain and, where necessary, regenerate these areas, so that the interests of the land and the people who depend directly upon that land come first. This formula combines the natural resources and natural beauty with human life. We need to strike a balance which will be true to Scottish need and idiom. The objectives of such parks should be not only the conserving of a valuable part of Scotland's heritage for future generations, but the development of a national organisation which would provide the wide range of required skills of practical and theoretical management. The stated objectives should be harmonised with the programmes of the NCC in nature conservation and the CCS in conservation of amenity. The complexity of the planning and administration system involving several central and local government bodies, many voluntary conservation bodies and many more user bodies is in itself one of the great threats to the life of a 'National Park' revival in Scotland. The planning system is caught in a bureaucratic straightjacket of its own making.

It is interesting to note that in the earlier discussion on National Parks, five sites were selected. Knoydart was one of two others held in reserve. There are two reasons for this; firstly, at that time the criteria that were being applied were different from what is now suggested; secondly, at that time areas like Knoydart were believed to be so remote as to be impregnable. There is nowhere in Scotland, nor in the world, of which that can be said today.

(b) Suspected pollution in the Bonnybridge/Denny area: waste incineration and public anxiety

The controversy in the Bonnybridge/Denny area arose soon after Re-Chem International began operating their incinerator plant there in early 1975. Local residents complained about nuisance caused by smoke, smell and eye irritation. A petition was sent to the Scottish Office; Re-Chem held two public meetings; it was accepted by the Company that stack emissions were causing a nuisance; accordingly the stack was heightened in 1976.

In 1978 Re-Chem was fined for allowing noxious vapour to be released and a local nurseryman was awarded £3000 damages by a Falkirk court because crop damage on his land was held to have been caused by the fumes. In the same year it was reported that a local farmer had lost 37 cattle in 18 months. A veterinary investigation subsequently attributed these deaths to ragwort (a common toxic plant with a brilliant yellow flower) poisoning. Another farmer had problems for several years from 1980 with cattle summer-grazed near the plant. According to Press Reports a number of disorders developed. Calves were born blind or deformed and milk yields fell drastically. In 1983, 45 cows were culled by being either sold or slaughtered. A newspaper account stated that some 110 cows and 70 calves were lost in 1984. The veterinary diagnosis attributed the problems with this farmer's cattle to 'fat cow syndrome', a nutritional imbalance. The farmer rejected this diagnosis.

Various surveys and tests were carried out in the area by the Department of Agriculture, the Agricultural College and HM Industrial Inspectorate. Many other bodies and individuals were also involved and expertise was sought concerning the chemical assessment of samples for the presence of the highly toxic polychlorinated biphenyls (PCB's), which, have been linked with cancer, and dioxins near the plant. If PCB's are not incinerated at a high enough temperature, the extremely dangerous dioxins can be produced. Knowledge of this and the incident in Seveso in Italy in 1976 when dioxins were released into the environment increased the anxiety of local people about human health. Concern over the incidence of cancer and the occurrence of eye defects in two babies in the immediate area led to the setting up of the Independent Review Group by the Scottish Secretary. Demands for a full public enquiry were rejected.

Although the Re-Chem plant had closed in 1984, protest continued. In November 1985, the local MP, Mr Denis Canavan, and the MEP for mid-Scotland and Fife, Mr Alex Falconer, were reported to be stepping up the campaign for a wide ranging public enquiry. Dr Wills, Mr Falconer's research assistant had been compiling a dossier on Re-Chem's operations. This had formed the basis of Parliamentary questions and questions in Strasbourg. In January 1986 Re-Chem launched a vigorous rebuttal of statements and claims made in the dossier material. Mr Falconer is reported as saying that 'The 125-page Summary of our file has been sent to the new Scottish Secretary'. Clearly the matter is far from settled.

The report of the Review Group (the *Lenihan Report*) was published in February 1985. Subsequently headlines in the press appeared, such as 'Study fails to link Re-Chem to toxins', and 'Chemical plant not to blame for diseases'. However, despite reassurances from Government sources, fears were not allayed, nor was the principal farmer in the controversy satisfied. The report maintained that there is nothing unusual about the general state of human, animal or plant health in the Bonnybridge/Denny area. Mortality and cancer registration data for the area were found to be normal. However, the incidence of the congenital anomaly, microphthalmas (smallness of the eye) in babies in the Forth Valley Health Board area was 'sufficiently striking' to warrant further investigation in the Board's area and elsewhere. The report stated that the levels of PCB's, dioxins and furans in cattle and soil in the area were not unusually high. The Group had 'no evidence which implicates the Re-Chem plant' in the problems on the farm thought to be principally affected. Nothing abnormal was found as regards plant morbidity.

One important comment contained in the Report is that 'there are many other potential sources of pollution in the Bonnybridge/Denny area apart from Re-Chem'. The Report concluded with the significant statement that 'there is a need for more effective dissemination of reliable information and knowledgeable guidance on sources, health effects and background levels of potentially harmful substances in the environment . . .'.

Comment

The nature of an industrial society is such that waste, including toxic wastes, must be disposed of. There is a growing appreciation that dumping of waste either at sea or on land does not necessarily dispose of it. The sea is not a limitless dustbin, but a global commons whose ecology is profoundly affected by man's activities. On land the persistence of some chemicals, or their contamination of ground water can result in problems in the future. 'Safe' methods of destruction (by incineration for example) are only as safe as their consistent standard of operation allows them to be and even occasional lapses in standards of maintenance or of operation can have grave consequences. It is tempting, however where a suspicion of damaging pollution exists, to blame the most obvious cause. The nature of enquiry into such incidents tends to be (or to be made to be by the media and other interests) adversarial. This may lead to lack of disclosure and frankness by the personnel involved. Where the local community insists that a strong *prima facie* case exists, it is essential that immediate steps should be taken publicly, to ensure that the issue is investigated promptly, thoroughly and impartially. Official resistance to such legitimate concern can only increase local anxieties and undermine public confidence.

In the case discussed above, no positive conclusions have been reached. Consideration of these problems lies at the limits of scientific knowledge. A complete understanding of the events described may never be reached. The most immediate source of anxiety to the local community, the Re-Chem plant, has now been closed down (although there have been worries over the demolition of the incinerator chimney and furnaces). But to consider the matter closed, may be an ostrich-like attitude; the problems attributed to Re-Chem may have been from the action of other industrial activity or, as the enquiries have suggested, they may spring from a variety of quite different causes. It is hoped that Bonnybridge will have no further similar incidents, but the problems of the safe disposal of toxic wastes and of identifying the fundamental causes of local environmental health problems or damage to plants or animals remains with us. It is not sufficient to say 'not in my back yard'.

(c) Caithness/Sutherland.
Rapid afforestation of a major wildlife habitat

An area of 189000 hectares in Sutherland and Caithness, stretching from Ben Loyal to Wick, is described as 'flow Country'. It consists largely of an undulating boggy plateau, not exceeding 250 metres in height.

This area already has substantial conifer plantations. The total area owned by forestry interests is 65000 hectares, of this 39000 have been planted or is proposed for planting. (The Forestry Commission owns 23500 hectares, of which 18000 are planted or to be planted, private forestry interests own or manage 42000 hectares, of which 21000 are planted or to be planted.) There are nine SSSIs with a total area of 10900 hectares. A Nature Reserve of 49 hectares exists in Strathy Bog.

The area is a unique habitat for a range of uncommon species of bird, and this habitat would be largely destroyed by the proposed increase of forestry.

Some forestry interests have suggested that this 'empty' area is well suited for large scale development, and that despite the problems of soil, bog and wind, commercial crops of timber can be produced with modern techniques. Others have expressed doubts about the use of such exposed sites and have suggested that a commercially unacceptable time-cycle will be required to produce a crop.

There have already been serious problems in the area due to infestation of Forestry Commission plantations of lodge pole pine by pine beauty moth. The high cost of aerial spraying is cited as a major economic disadvantage and there are some objections to this type of control for environmental reasons. Concern has also been expressed that there will be problems of acidification, run off and particularly, windthrow (deep ploughing is being used).

Those who oppose both the speed and the scale of the change of land-use consider that the plateau area should be left untouched, but agree that some forestry is appropriate and could be developed around the boundaries of the area, on the drier slopes dropping into the straths.

The dispute is clear-cut in that the argument is between commercial forestry interests who wish to develop the area and nature conservationists who wish to preserve it. But it becomes more complex when the arguments of the opponents are examined. They claim that even if planting were acceptable on this site, conditions will prevent a successful crop. While the damage done, especially by ploughing, is irreversible. The existence of SSSIs gives some protection, but their area is small and it has been said that the rules governing SSSIs have already been broken. A conflict of this type may not be reconcilable, but a decision has not yet been reached as to how and by whom such issues should be examined and adjudicated, so that the interests involved can all feel that their opinions have been properly considered.

(d) Central Scotland –
the regeneration of post-industrial land

The upland area on both sides of the Edinburgh/Glasgow motorway (M8), stretching north to Falkirk and south to the Pentland Hills has suffered a century of economic and social decline. The area was the site of the shale oil industry which left a legacy of industrial dereliction. There is considerable pollution from industry in the west, from the oil refinery and from two coal-fired power stations. Nine thousand hectares, half the industrially derelict land in Scotland, were estimated to exist in Central Scotland in 1975. It was windswept and with virtually no topographic shelter.

During the 1960s the Forestry Commission established substantial conifer plantations in a wide band along the southern side of the region (Breich, Fauldhouse, Carluke), and this area was expanded so that by 1975 the area planted totalled 3500 hectares. Since 1970 private landowners have added 2400 hectares of coniferous trees. Successful experiments have been made to establish vegetation on waste bings. The creation of plantations has encountered problems, particularly of fire and of windthrow.

In 1977 the Central Scotland Woodlands Project (CSWP) was set up, on the proposal of Lothian Regional Council (as 'a positive way of overcoming the environmental blight associated with the area') by the Countryside Commission and the three Regions involved. Its objectives, broadly, were to improve the landscape of the area and thus the amenity of the population, to make more use of marginal land for afforestation and to establish shelter belts where appropriate. In six years it has encouraged a multitude of planting schemes, mainly small in scale, in open spaces and on derelict sites, using broadleaved trees. Over 500 hectares have been established through CSWP efforts. The benefits in terms of amenity are substantial and the involvement of residents, especially young people, has been most successful. A 'Farmers' Tree Scheme' has now been launched to help establish or improve shelter belts, both for the shelter of crops and stock, but also as a potential commercial activity for the farmer.

In addition to the CSWP, the Scottish Development Agency and the New Town Development Corporations of Cumbernauld and Livingston have between them planted 500 hectares. The overall increase in productive afforestation since 1960 is from less than 4 per cent of the land area to more than 10 per cent.

The Community Opportunities West Lothian (COWL) Project was set up in 1983, with the object of creating forest walks, parkland areas and ponds, and generally improving the forests' attractiveness.

Developments in this area are encouraging and are an outstanding example of co-operation between different authorities and organisations – three Regions, six District Councils, the Forestry Commission, the Nature Conservancy Council, the Countryside Commission, the SDA, New Town Development Corporations, private landowners and farmers.

A valuable resource of timber has been established, which once maturity has been reached, it has been estimated, will produce 50000 tons timber per year, close to major potential markets. It has been stated that there are substantial areas suitable for planting – both for commercial plantations and as shelter belts, further integrating forestry and farming. The pioneer work of the CSWP can be further developed for many amenity and recreational projects. Wildlife, already on the increase from a depressingly low base in the 1950s, will benefit from the steady improvement of habitats. The whole environment and social wellbeing of the area is being steadily improved.

(e) Lurcher's Gully –
The siting and effect of skiing developments

Downhill skiing has developed in Scotland since the Second World War in three centres – Cairn Gorm, Glencoe and Glenshee. More recently a fourth centre at the Lecht on the Cockbridge to Tomintoul road has been opened. The growth of skiing on Cairn Gorm has been accompanied by the establishment of substantial tourist facilities at Aviemore. Towards the end of the 1970s, the non-profit making company responsible for operating the chair lift and ski tows, put forward a project suggesting that skiing should be introduced into the three corries to the west of the present area. The scheme included ski lifts, shelter huts, restaurant/snack bars and a mile of new road with a car park. The proposal was supported by the Highland Regional Council and by the Highlands and Islands Development Board, which owns and leases the present site.

The area is the upper part of the Glenmore Forest Park which is the most important tourist asset in the district of Badenoch and Strathspey. It is contiguous with the unique and internationally important Cairn Gorm Nature Reserve. The whole area is designated as a National Scenic Area by the Countryside Commission for Scotland. The intention of the proposed development was to expand the winter tourist season to enable the tourist facilities, only fully used during a short summer season, to be better employed. It was suggested that concentration in this area would result in further development in Speyside and would create a centre capable of competing with Continental resorts. The lack of a sufficient number of slopes for beginners, for example, had become a serious matter.

There was immediate opposition from a number of conservation bodies. The NCC expressed concern about the erosion of soil and vegetation, disturbance to wildlife, increasing amounts of litter and damage to the area. The CCS suggested that the scheme was premature before alternatives had been examined. They pointed out that the areas proposed for additional tows have a scenic quality and remote character which is enjoyed by walkers and climbers throughout the year.

It was stated that the present development had already seriously, and perhaps irrevocably, damaged neighbouring land. In particular, the existence of the ski lift had allowed access to the plateau in greater numbers than the area could sustain, resulting in serious erosion and the litter deposited had encouraged gulls and crows to scavenge high on the mountainside. When litter was not available they had turned their attention to the rare birds in the reserve. The actual skiing areas were heavily eroded, damaging the appearance of the area in summer and producing a change in the drainage pattern resulting in more flash floods causing damage in the downstream areas. This would escalate if further development was allowed.

Those opposed to the development did so on these grounds, but also produced evidence that the area did not provide sufficient snow cover. They insisted that developments in other areas on a smaller scale would provide more competition and more economic benefits overall, and suggested that concentration in one area could have damaging social effects both on the locality and on other communities in upper Speyside. The erratic nature of the weather and snowfall in Scotland made it more sensible to have a geographical spread of ski developments, and would offer benefits to other communities. They suggested that the long-term success of tourist development demanded the protection of the basic resource that attracts the visitor – the scenery and the wildlife – and the preservation of a wide variety of recreational opportunities. The new road envisaged would traverse the mountain at 2000 feet and in blizzards could have grave escape problems. The proposers of the scheme responded to some objections. They suggested that the road would be closed in summer to restrict tourist pressure on the new area. They announced that all hardware for the new installations would be placed by helicopter.

The project was supported by the Highland Region 'to create a large integrated downhill skiing facility with a stronger likelihood of stimulating the long-stay midweek market'. Grampian Region realised that they would be faced with serious environmental consequences without corresponding economic advantages, and therefore opposed it. A number of skiing and sports organisations were strongly in favour (their support, it was suggested, was stronger the less knowledge they had of local weather conditions).

A public enquiry was held at Kingussie commencing in September 1981. The Secretary of State rejected the Lurcher's Gully proposal in December 1982 and proposed the introduction of new guidelines 'in order to reduce the future scope for conflict in any part of Scotland between skiing development proposals and other forms of land use'. As part of the new national planning guidelines series, he proposed 'to draw up generalised locations where such developments could take place and for the local authorities to then define specific sites in their local plans after consultation with interested parties'. These guidelines were issued in July 1984. They defined Cairn Gorm, Glenshee, Glencoe and the Lecht as 'primary', with Drumochter, Newtonmore, Fort William and Ben Wyvis as 'secondary' skiing areas.

A new development was proposed for Jean's Gully, Drumochter in February 1984. Contrary to advice given by the Nature Conservancy Council and the Scottish Wild Life Trust, this was approved by the Secretary of State.

Downhill skiing tends to monopolise the land-use of that particular area and to conflict with other recreational uses, nor is it easy to avoid serious effects to the local ecology; its extension is therefore regarded with considerable caution by those who have a reverence for the land and its natural inhabitants. On the other hand skiing is a healthy and wholesome activity which should be encouraged as an enjoyable outlet for the energies of a largely urban population. The question to be resolved is whether a reasonable expansion of the present facilities can be made without serious environmental consequences. It has been suggested that the Kingussie enquiry was conducted on too narrow a basis and that the real question of Scotland's failure to learn from the experience of mountain management of other countries was hardly addressed. Despite this, it seems that a sensible decision was reached and that the introduction of planning guidelines represents a positive approach for the future. However the serious problem of over-use of the Cairn Gorm plateau remains unsolved.

(f) The Western Isles Integrated Development Programme

The Outer Hebrides have a total population of 30000. Apart from the town of Stornoway with 8000 inhabitants, most of the population lives on the coastal fringes, many in the typical linear crofting townships. The total area is approximately 300000 hectares of which over 70 per cent is under crofting tenure. There are approximately 6000 crofts, with only 24000 hectares of in bye land and 188000 hectares of common grazing. Ninety per cent of agricultural income comes from the breeding and rearing of beef cattle and sheep but other sources of income, particularly fishing have been usual. There has been a steady decline in the viability of crofting and fishing and limited opportunities of employment in the services sector, with, as a result, a constantly high level of unemployment.

The area was selected as one of three pilot Integrated Development Programmes (IDPs) of the EEC, and was designed 'to improve the socio-economic structure of regions where although agriculture is of no little importance, it cannot itself provide the population with a reasonable standard of living'.

The UK Government set up certain objectives. The first were to improve pastures for summer grazing and to increase the production of winter keep. At the same time it was hoped to improve the quality of breeding cattle and sheep (to produce a higher market value). An appropriate marketing development was also required. Fisheries were to be developed, diversified and extended and fish farming was to be encouraged. The infrastructure, in particular transport systems and water supplies had to be improved. Certain wealth generating activities based on indigenous resources were also to be promoted.

The programme initially proposed UK public expenditure of £20 million over five years for agricultural and fisheries development. The Community Farm Fund (FEOGA) would refund 40 per cent of this amount. Expenditure on infrastructure and related factors, was estimated at £36 million, again to be spent over a five year period and some EEC grants were available to set against this.

The announcement of the IDP was vigorously opposed by some conservationists. They were particularly concerned that the agricultural land improvement measures within the programme posed a serious threat to the important wildlife habitats of the Western Isles, particularly those of the lime rich machair.

While the governing EEC regulation required that the programme should include 'an assurance that the actions envisaged are compatible with the protection of the environment', such were the limitations of agricultural policy, both within the EEC and the UK, that this fell very far short of the integration of environmental protection measures within the programme, as it was argued that agricultural funds could not be used for this purpose. Thus while administrative arrangements were made for taking environmental advice on land improvement and fish farming projects, the cost of providing this service was not met out of the programme funds, subject to EEC reimbursement, but had to be met by the Nature Conservancy Council. There was the added drawback that the advice was only sought after the individual project had been formulated and grant had been applied for, so that it came to be regarded as a resented limitation on development aspirations. In essence the project assessment and monitoring programmes funded by the NCC were an 'added on' rather than an integral part of the programme and so inevitably took the form of a negative control rather than being developed as an opportunity for environmental improvement by the IDP project team.

The Programme came into operation on 1st September 1982. After three years it has been said that 'evidence of its impact can be seen all over the islands in the form of fish and shellfish farms in the sea lochs and areas of improved grassland'; 3500 participants have made a total of 12500 applications for land improvement grants and there have been 87 participants in fish farming schemes. Applications have covered 55 per cent of the total land holdings.

Grants approved for land improvement have greatly exceeded the original estimates. At first the emphasis was on preliminary works, particularly fencing, but over the three years the trend has been towards grassland improvement. Grants have also been made for drainage, buildings, machinery and horticulture. The cattle improvement scheme has been successful and improved numbers and quality can be seen in the traditional cattle breeding areas of the islands. There does not appear to have been an increase in cattle numbers in the predominantly sheep breeding areas, in spite of the possibilities arising from the improved pastures. There have been fewer participants in the sheep improvement scheme than was expected, probably because the requirements of the scheme do not conform with the production and sale of store and fat lambs which is the growing emphasis of sheep breeders. The improvements in marketing and transport are of great importance and both have been substantially assisted by the programme. Since its inception £564000 has been provided as grant assistance for transport, marketing and slaughtering facilities. Expenditure on developing fish farms has been considerable; a total of nearly £3 million having been involved. In addition grants totalling £1.4 million have been made for fish processing and marketing. Infrastructure developments include new ferry terminals, road improvements and sea defence works.

The most interesting features of the IDP have been its insistence on developing transport and marketing alongside agricultural improvement and the encouragement of the development of other sources of income by the crofters. It has also been important that the whole community has been made aware of the purpose and progress of the Programme and considerable effort has gone into communications and public relations. It appears that the benefits of the Programme have been spread quite evenly over the whole area.

While the worst fears of the environmentalists concerning the possible adverse effects of the IDP have not, and are unlikely to be realised, experience has confirmed the unsatisfactoriness of the approach to conservation embodied in its 'added on' rather than integral character within the IDP. Partly as a result of Western Isles experience this seems to be becoming more generally recognised, as evidenced by the different approach being suggested for agricultural support in proposed 'Environmentally Sensitive Areas' where positive environmental conservation and improvement will be actively encouraged within the grant system and built into agricultural practices.

The geographical isolation of the Western Isles and its other special characteristics have, on the one had, made it an ideal site for this Programme, but on the other hand make it more difficult to use as a model for developments of a similar general nature elsewhere. There are, however valuable lessons to be learned from it which could well be applied to other parts of Scotland, both in terms of involving conservation considerations from the beginning, and in identifying the most successful elements of the programme.

6. SOME URGENT CONSIDERATIONS

This report does not attempt to reach conclusions, but offers some urgent questions which should be discussed widely. If the countryside which makes up 85 per cent of the total area of Scotland is to have a lively, industrious rural population and is to be handed down to our children in good condition, then answers to these questions have to be political, economic and social. Underlying them there has to be a better understanding of our stewardship and trusteeship of nature. Unless pressure for action is initiated now, the pace of change will exceed the capacity of Government and social institutions to cope with them; the inflexibility of political and economic systems is such, that before an effective response can be made, irreversible damage will have been done to the landscape, to wildlife and to the rural communities.

Afforestation

In the opinion of many informed people the need for planning control of afforestation is the most urgent question of land-use today. There are strong arguments that a further extension of planting is desirable, both to meet timber demand and to give useful employment to land (about two million hectares) some of which will be taken out of agricultural use because of surpluses in production. Major expansions are now being made by forestry management companies on behalf of institutions such as pension funds requiring long-term investments and private individuals seeking tax advantages. There is nothing illegal or unsound in these activities; the present planting grant and taxation system strongly favours these types of investment. The question is whether such a system is now and in the forseeable future desirable in the interests of the community and the land. The system lends itself to large scale blanket planting, sometimes of unfavourable sites and with little concern for the ecology of the area or for the local community, who may have no say in any afforestation proposals. The new owners of the land may have little or no contact with the land and lack any sense of history or altruism for the future of the land and the people. Planning of new plantations does not involve any elected body and management is left in the hands of competent companies whose interests are essentially commercial. The Forestry Commission can exercise only very limited control by modest conditions attached to planting grants; and these have been shown to be increasingly ineffective. There is an absence of public accountability for these forestry operations which are altering the face of Scotland with adverse effects on scenery, wildlife and community life.

There is a relatively new enthusiasm among politicians, administrators, farming organisations and conservationists to encourage forestry as an integrated part of farming, as is already the case in well run estates and is normal in most parts of continental Europe, but present systems in Britain are not yet geared to make the transition. A new mixed land-use policy is required to encourage farmers with the right financial and technical assistance. There is a strong body of public opinion which believes that a policy of integration can only succeed if planning includes both afforestation and agriculture, a view which has been hotly opposed for many years for reasons of democratic freedom. The case for control becomes stronger, however, if financial aids to farmers give them an opportunity for alternative earnings when their main source of income is declining. The present climate of Government opinion is against planning controls for reasons of cost, administrative over-burden and delay and an emphasis on the personal freedom of the land-owner. Nevertheless, the scale of development envisaged doubles the existing forest cover in a relatively short period. If carried out without careful control over where and how the new plantations are to be sited, irreversible damage will be done to the Scottish landscape. This is indeed a matter for national concern.

The pattern of land ownership in Scotland differs from that in other European countries in the number of large estates and in the crofting system. About 100 estates cover 25 per cent of the total land area: 37 per cent of the land is owned in estates of between 1000 and 8000 hectares and 25 per cent in farms of under 1000 hectares. The Forestry Commission owns 10 per cent of the land. Of the 35000 'farm units' in Scotland, 17000 are full time and 18000 are crofts or smallholdings, frequently operated on a part time basis.

The study of land ownership does not produce obvious conclusions. Some large estates are well managed with progressive policies of farming and forestry, good relationships with tenants and a sensitive attitude to conservation and wildlife. The best private forestry is in the large family estates run by resident owners who have well proportioned agro-forestry enterprises and have accepted management agreements for Nature Reserves and SSSIs. Other estates are owned by absentee landlords, and retained largely for sporting purposes, such as deer-stalking, shooting or fishing. Many estates have imperfect policies, for example, of control of red deer and an unwillingness to accept advice or responsibility on questions of land-use or conservation.

A growing area of Scotland is being purchased by institutions and individuals interested only in a long-term investment and by wealthy international businessmen or syndicates interested only in exploiting the 'sporting' aspect, sometimes in ways which do not conform to

Scottish traditions. The total percentage is small so far, but a fast rate of increase is likely. As was seen in the case of Knoydart, there are very few purchasers able to accept the long-term financial implications of responsibility for such a large area of land. There are grounds for believing that many estates are being under-managed and over-exploited; under-managed in that inadequate staff exist for the overall upkeep of the estate and over-exploited in carrying and even encouraging stocks of deer which are too high. On the agricultural side, inappropriate grazing systems by sheep are a cause for concern. More large properties will come on the market, and there is no sign of a wealthy class of responsible people in Britain willing to share and contribute to the vision of a regenerated Highlands and Islands. Nor is there any national body sufficiently endowed to do so. There is no simple solution to the problem of developing policies of responsible land-use in the remoter areas of Scotland. It is vital, however, that dramatic and irreversible changes such as blanket afforestation should not happen without proper consideration of the implications for the future.

Agriculture

The probability of rapid change in the economics of farming, due to changes in the CAP brings to an end a period of relative prosperity for Scottish farmers. Individual farmers struggling for economic survival do not concern themselves with questions of long-term sustainability. Some may be forced to sell their land, while others may adopt short-term policies which are not environmentally desirable. A likely result will be the afforestation of areas which will grow a crop of trees but which are unsuitable for forestry on environmental or social and cultural grounds. The inference is that, in Britain, a conservation-minded community must be a reasonably prosperous one; yet it seems obvious that there will be severe financial pressure on agriculture. It is uncertain how far this can be countered by finding other sources of income, through alternative land-use, principally in forestry, recreation, sporting and tourism. A vigorous response from a lively and self-confident industry can be expected, but the future wellbeing of farming must be a concern of the whole community. It must be recognised that the agricultural industry is the nation's provider of food, but that the growing of food may not in itself provide a sufficient income for future viability, especially in marginal areas.

It has to be repeated that a prosperous rural community is essential for the social health of Scotland and its prosperity must rest on a viable and vigorous agricultural industry made up of active working farmers. Farmers must, however, be prepared to operate in the interests of the whole community. This may involve some loss of freedom in the acceptance of planning control over land-use, but it might include a development of the principle established under the *Wild Life and Countryside Act* that nature conservation should become a commercial activity – a land-use in its own right – practised by the landowner on behalf of the whole community. Such a development demands creative imagination from all concerned and, of course, carries with it all the risks of abuse by unscrupulous individuals, though the Nature Conservancy Council should be able to deal with these. This is a critical time for the future of agriculture and it is necessary that priorities should be restated and the consequences accepted.

Pollution

Forty years after the end of the Second World War, an island in Gruinard Bay remains isolated, still contaminated by anthrax introduced during wartime experiments in biological warfare. It should become a site of national pilgrimage to remind us of what damage we can do to God's creation in our efforts, not to subjugate nature, but to destroy fellow men. Some problems of pollution today are even more alarming in their long-term consequences; the disposal of nuclear waste is by far the most serious. In some countries it has been treated casually, with consequences which have still to be fully realised, while in the UK, although, on the whole, a more responsible policy has been followed, there are areas of grave concern – and a need for the most rigorous monitoring and control of developments.

On the general question of pollution, much important work has been done by the Royal Commission on Environmental Pollution set up in 1970. Its remit is '. . .to advise on matters, both national and international, concerning the pollution of the environment; on the adequacy of research in this field; and the future possibilities of danger to the environment'. As a body independent of Government it has seen its role as not only to advise Government but to inform the general public. Its advice has had a major influence on Government action and attitudes; it is unfortunate that the contents of its eleven reports are not more widely known.

Despite the broadly effective framework for pollution control developed in this country there are inevitably issues that arise which cause deep public concern. Statements such as 'there is no scientific evidence' do not convince a community that sees, or believes it sees, actual physical evidence. The scientific proof, linking cause and effect, may be difficult or impossible to establish; combinations of circumstances may not be understood; the basic reason for the unease may not have been sufficiently considered. Public attitudes may vary widely and may include different elements – fear of lost employment; anxiety about major, albeit unlikely, disaster;

concern for the health of children and for future generations of children.

Much effort is spent not to resolve pollution problems, but to have them transferred elsewhere, geographically or to future generations. This attitude is understandable, but surely not justifiable, and is to be challenged. The problem of acid rain has been described in Chapter 4. This major issue has caused profound anger in Norway and Sweden at the UK Government's refusal to join the '30% club' of European countries. The attitude of the Central Electricity Generating Board is that the damage alleged to be caused by acid rain is less significant than has been reported; that other factors may be involved; and that cost of reducing emissions is not justified by the potential results. 'It is throwing a billion dollar solution at a million dollar problem'. This has proved quite unacceptable to informed Scandinavian opinion, 'Alas the CEGB is still intent on acting against the public interest – the same shirking of responsibility, the same partial presentation of evidence and obfuscation of the issues, the same complacent lack of concern noted by the Select Committee are still in obvious evidence'.

Research and Development

In a period when major changes in agriculture, forestry and other forms of land-use are certain, it is disquieting to learn of the cuts in DAFS research and development funding of £4 million, fully operational in 1987/8. Cuts will affect both Scottish Agricultural Research Institutes and the Agricultural Colleges. In addition, the Advisory Services face swingeing cuts of 41 per cent from April 1987, at a time when their valuable services in assisting farmers to cope with change will be particularly necessary.

The severe reductions in funding of Universities and Research Institutes already experienced and still to be

felt is well known. The need for well-directed programmes of research in widely different fields such as for
example, the implications of possible climatic shifts, the
effects of the integration of farming and forestry, or to
develop a better understanding of lower input farming,
cannot be over-emphasised.

It is hoped that despite the severe financial pressures,
a proper emphasis will be given to the need for fundamental research, along with a proper balance of research
and development directed at the practical problems of
land-use for a sustainable future.

7. SCOTLAND'S RESPONSIBILITY FOR WORLD HUNGER

It is estimated that at least 400 million people in the World do not have enough food for health and for the survival of their children. In areas of extreme vulnerability to droughts and floods, hunger and malnutrition may give way to mass starvation. Such a famine in Africa and South East Asia has held a dominant place in television and radio programmes and in the newspapers during the past year. The magnitude of the public's response stands in contrast to the seemingly half-hearted response of the Governments of the EEC. The question is therefore continually being asked, 'Why is the European food surplus not made available for the starving of the world, and why do we talk of quotas and other means of cutting European production when half the world has not enough to eat?' In a report on Land-Use in Scotland it is important that this question should be addressed and that Scotland's responsibility as part of Europe should be considered.

The deplorable world food situation is the result of many factors. So far as the developing world is concerned, these include:

(1) Agricultural systems, in many countries, of a non-sustainable nature, for example through:

    (i) the use of inappropriate systems of arable farming in a fragile environment;

   (ii) the destruction of forests, either for fuel or for commercial purposes;

  (iii) the over-use of marginal land due to population pressures, or the progressive increase of land used for cash crops.

(2) The best agricultural land in many cases being taken by commercial, often transnational firms, for cash crops for export, including coffee, tea, fruit and textile fibres.

(3) The markets and the prices of important exports of developing countries, including sugar and oil seeds, being undermined by Europe's own production with the support of protectionist policies.

(4) The international debt crisis caused, initially by the rise in oil prices coinciding with, and partly triggered by, a fall in World commodity prices, and a fall in World Trade.

(5) Severe drought conditions in a band across sub-Saharan Africa to South East Asia and in parts of Southern Africa. This has forced many people to become refugees and they have found themselves caught up in political conflicts as well as natural disasters. With encroaching desertification, re-habilitation of the land and of the people is increasingly difficult.

While short-term aid for people *in extremis* is clearly a responsibility in which Christians must share, it would be a mistake to allow this type of assistance to be seen as our main commitment to helping to alleviate the problem. Those closest to the tragedy have warned that the continuing supply of food may do more harm than good in a subsistence economy; in order to survive in their harsh environment, the people must return to their land to re-establish their farming systems. Food aid channelled through emergency relief centres does not in itself get people back on the land growing crops and providing for their own livelihoods. At worst, the available food supplies may discourage the sowing of crops, push down prices to farmers and further reduce the incentive to produce. Delay in responding to needs can aggravate this problem if food arrives too late in the season to avert famine deaths, but then becomes available at the time when local farmers are trying to sell their own produce from the following crop.

The response of the major industrialised countries of Europe and North America should therefore include efforts to develop better systems to allow stocks of grain to be held, always available, with arrangements for efficient transport and swift distribution to areas of particular need. The necessary quantities to maintain such stocks should be included in EEC planning and we should only talk about surpluses when a reserve to deal with the food crises of the world has been included in the annual target figure, but developing such reserves does not absolve Northern countries from further responsibilities. It is only a first step towards adjusting our agricultural policies and practices to the long-term requirements for meeting World food needs on a sustainable basis. Foremost among these requirements is an ethic of stewardship in the management of natural resources, and in this respect the industrialised countries have fallen a long way short. Our approaches to technology and resource use in agriculture, as elsewhere, have had a powerful impact on the strategies adopted in the developing world. This impact is felt through scientific research, through technical education, through aid agencies and international organisations, through the products of international firms producing agro-chemicals and machinery, and through the market pressures of the world economy. Sometimes the effects are positive, but too often they are negative and in some instances disastrous. Transferred to environments with irregular rainfall regimes, a greater abundance of insect species, climatic conditions favourable to the multiplication of pest problems, and often fragile soils, the flaws in our own approaches to agricultural modernisation have shown up much more quickly and with far more adverse effects than in cool temperate conditions. We have tended to assume that fertility can be purchased out of a polythene bag, that pest problems can be overcome simply by increasing the use of pesticides, that the soil can be treated as little more than a medium for transporting water-soluable nutrients to the growing plant.

These approaches have brought apparent gains, at least in the short-term, not only in Europe and North America, but also in some parts of the tropics. There is, at the same time, abundant evidence of the limitations, both economic and ecological; much of the World cannot afford to take this road, and there are growing pressures to re-examine the goals of our own technical innovations in farming. In so doing, we may at the same time contribute something towards meeting the challenge of achieving durable solutions to the world food problems. In addition it has to be recognised that two other factors determine why land which should be growing food is being used to grow cash crops. Firstly, the international financial system is designed and operated by, and for the benefit of, the Northern half of the world; secondly, the populations of the Northern countries demand a widely varied diet and other commodities. The implications are considerable for our life styles, and thier effect on our agriculture if they were taken seriously would be significant.

8. FINAL REFLECTIONS ON RESPONSIBILITY

This report has been concerned with Christian responsibility in land-use in relation to the diversity of our Scottish inheritance and the varieties of interest and attitude among present users. But what is responsibility? The Victorians tended to think of it as a duty to be performed, which could be clearly delineated from the beginning. Yet to be responsible only out of duty seems now to be a cold, limited and extraneous way to behave. It is not so much the case that we have a duty towards God and the land as that we have a continuing relationship with both, while responsibility is the moral aspect of these relationships as they take place. Where no relationship is acknowledged, or where it is so warped that it has lost its mutuality; waste, destruction or maltreatment are possible, and no responsibility is perceived. This has happened and could still happen in Scottish land-use. Conversely, it is where such relationships are acknowledged and enjoyed that their best possible maintenance is responsibly sought. All enduring relationships of whatever kind, have to be worked through – they do not simply happen. For this reason the report began by affirming the relationship of humanity and all creation with its creator, and the further relationships of humanity with non-human creation in the roles of responsible steward, trustee and companion.

Relationships are not static things: they change over time with the variety of situations in which they flourish. Responsibility, therefore, the moral aspect of such relationships, cannot be minutely prescribed beforehand as if it were a constant which could be universally applied in any circumstances whatsoever. Instead it means finding the right thing to do or to be in the particular time and circumstances in which we find ourselves now. As H. R. Niebuhr has written: 'for the ethics of responsibility the fitting action, the one that fits into a total interaction as response and as anticipation of further response, is alone conducive to the good and alone is right' (*The Responsible Self* p. 61). Responsibility in land-use, then is to find the action which best fits our steward, trustee and companion relationship in a particular situation with all its contingent individual characteristics, and which will allow that relationship to continue.

Afforestation with a single species, such as Sitka Spruce, meets the condition of our role as steward very well in some places, but that does not mean a blanket approval of planting on every site, nor does it indicate approval of all techniques used. We are also trustees of the variety of tree species in Scotland and this involves the preservation and rehabilitation of the remnants of our native pine forest and of the existing broadleaved woodlands. In all new projects we should underline the importance of landscape in the layout. Short-term instrumental value is always the most obvious and apparently compelling, especially to those who profit by it, but for true responsibility the negative effects of any proposal have to be weighed and the whole matter set in a wider context of other values. As trustees we should be concerned to encourage the development of new broadleaved plantations, and to overcome the financial constraints that tend to force growers into a shorter-term conifer crop on land suitable for broadleaved cultivation. We are also companions with the rest of creation, sharing our journey through time with them, and here our relationship is with wildlife in its intrinsic value with a moral standing in decisions and with importance to God. Wildlife can flourish in young spruce forests before the tree cover grows too dense, so the development of a rotation rather than the planting of an entire area is to be preferred.

In such ways as these, values can be implemented and the continuation of relationships responsibly undertaken, although some areas of decision are more difficult than others. But the better outcome will not happen unless there is a public awareness of the issues and a public outcry when commercial interests or individual thoughtlessness threaten prized values. Church members in their relationship with all creation and the God whose World this is are well placed to make that outcry responsibly.

The renewed sense of responsibility to the land, however, is occurring at a time when Scotland is riddled with unemployment. It may therefore appear callous to call for consideration of ecological systems and natural beauty when jobs could be created by some development. This objection has been raised on many issues, such as tourist developments or the siting of new chemical plants. Environmental groups have been accused of caring more for alpine flora or wild geese than for the livelihood of local people. That is a serious charge and not one to be dismissed lightly since we have responsible relations with each other as well as with the country we live in. Each instance has to be considered on its own merits, but it is our responsibility to see that the interests of creatures who cannot represent themselves are taken into consideration. Otherwise we relinquish our companion role except for sentimental occasions which cost us nothing. Further, in any situation there is more at stake than employment, even when things are as bad as they are. Among other matters there is also the future to be considered and the conditions among which our children and grandchildren will grow up.

For this reason, Livingston Development Corporation made a significant decision in 1985 by declining to have a chemical processing factory sited in their area because the community had demonstrated that they believed that there were risks for the health and safety of the surrounding area. The decision was taken in the emotionally charged atmosphere which followed the Bhopal disaster, and it may be that the particular plant proposed did not involve a significant risk. The fact remains that at a time when encouragement of new industry and the development of new employment is of the highest priority in every community, one community chose to put health, safety and clean air even higher. Employment at any cost cannot be justifiable and one of the areas of debate about cost must be that concerning land-use. Although unemployment is vicious, it remains a relevant question in every proposed case, 'what will this development do to the environment?' for our heirs, if not ourselves, may suffer the consequences. It is a worthwhile aim on quite prudential grounds to leave the World at least no more polluted than we found it.

The responsibility in view thus far has been action in response to moves already taking place, but responsibility for the future goes further than that, since particular proposals are generally instances of strategies, often devised outside Scotland and frequently so bound by red tape on arrival here that they are hard to challenge on the site. Planning for land-use in the forseeable future thus enters our sphere of responsibility. There is a sense in which Church members are unlikely to affect the Common Agricultural Policy of the EEC, the development of international corporations, the investments of pension funds, the policy of national Government or the preferences of wealthy estate owners, though local planning may be more manageable. And yet, in a number of ways, local grass-root voices may be heard. Indeed, the state of the environment has gone onto the international agenda because people everywhere, not only those with expertise or influential positions, have voiced their concern. It is now seen to be an issue which has to be taken into account on all occasions and is not the expression of local idiosyncracy. In that case it may not be worthwhile, for instance, for a company to attempt to locate in the teeth of informed local environmental opposition, or at least some compromise may be reached. Moreover, a Government which supports the Nature Conservancy Council cannot with ease permit developments which go against a conservation policy warmly endorsed by the public.

For that argument to be effective, however, public endorsement must include the work of the NCC in establishing and maintaining trusteeship in action. Farmers, foresters, ecologists, members of pension funds and so forth have the responsibility of keeping the issues firmly before the relevant decision-making bodies in their planning. The fact that the Church expresses its interest in, and backing for such moves may provide encouragement for individuals and a focal point for discussing the issues. Thus in spite of undoubted difficulties, the Church, through its members may have an influence on the ethos of future policy.

One of the most urgent messages of our time on every issue is that we live in one World. It is a message about the distribution of means and goods between rich and poor countries; it is a message about the danger of nuclear weapons, whoever may strike first. Again in this report the message is that we humans in Scotland live in one world of limited resources with all animate and inanimate creation, while the effects of our actions may be as irreversible here as in the other cases. It would be possible for Church members to try to escape from the complexity and responsibility of these issues by insisting that the total role of religion is to give spiritual comfort to the inner being of individuals. But in that case the Church and the World become two worlds, one devoted to God, the other left to the devil, so to speak. It is therefore important to insist that the Church is in the one World. On the one hand the Christian message of love and reconciliation is effective not only on some private spiritual or ecclesiastical aspect of people, but on the whole man or woman. It therefore affects, and gives direction to, all that men and women do, in Church or out of it. On the other hand the entire physical globe is dependent on God for its existence while every particle and the entire biosphere has importance to him. There is one World, on which Christian beliefs give a special perspective. There is one World which is the World God loves. Therefore responsible land-use is a religious issue.

REFERENCES

E. Ashby, *Reconciling Man with the Environment*. OUP (1978)

Robin Attfield, *The Ethics of Environmental Concern*. Blackwell (1983)

John Black, *The Dominion of Man*. EUP (1970)

John Calvin, *Commentaries on the First Book of Moses called Genesis*, Volume I, Calvin Translation Society (1847)

John Dickie, *The Organism of Christian Truth*. James Clarke (1930)

George S. Hendry, *Theology of Nature*. The Westminster Press (1980)

Aldo Leopold, *A Sand County Almanack with Other Essays on Conservation*. OUP (1966)

Alan E. Lewis, *Theatre of the Gospel*. Handsel Press (1984)

J. E. Lovelock, *Gaia. A New Look at Life on Earth*. OUP (1979)

J. Moltmann, *The Future of Creation*. SCM (1985)
God In Creation. SCM (1985)

H. Montefiore (ed), *Man and Nature*. Collins (1975)

A. R. Peacocke, *Creation and the World of Science*. Clarendon (1979)

Peter Singer, *Animal Liberation: A New Ethic for our Treatment of Animals*. Cape (1976)
'Utilitarianism and Vegetarianism', *Philosophy and Public Affairs*. (1980) pp. 325-37

Lynn White Jnr. 'The Historical Roots of Our Ecological Crisis.' *Science* **155**. (1967) 1203-7

Rene Dubos, *The Wooing of the Earth*. (1980)

A. V. Hill, *The Ethical Dilemma of Science, and other writings*. (1960)

SUGGESTIONS FOR FURTHER READING

C. Clapperton (ed), *Scotland; a New Study*. David and Charles (1985)

World Conservation Strategy. IUCN (1980)

The Conservation and Development Programme for the UK. A Response to the World Conservation Strategy. Kogan Page (1983). (esp. Chapter 8: R. J. Berry, Environmental Ethics and Conservation Action.)

Reports of the Royal commission on Environmental Pollution. HMSO

Fred Halliday (ed), *Wildlife of Scotland*. Macmillan (1979)

Wildlife and Countryside Act. HMSO (1981)

A Park System for Scotland. Countryside Commission for Scotland (1974)

F. F. Darling and J. Morton Boyd, *The Highlands and Islands*. Collins (1964)

SOCIETY, RELIGION AND TECHNOLOGY PROJECT

The Society, Religion and Technology Project exists to open up the processes of technical and social change to Christian scrutiny. Established in 1970, it seeks an informed understanding of the technical and social forces which are shaping the future.

Aware that ordinary people are often perplexed by new developments in science, technology and society, the Project acts as an interpreter, encouraging the practical outworking of Christian principles in the life of individuals, Churches and society.

The Project has a full-time Director who initiates research areas and who assists the many people who voluntarily give of their time to take part in study groups. Together, they function as a 'think-tank', a forum for policy debate and a resource for adult Christian education.

OTHER SRT PROJECT PUBLICATIONS

Not in My Backyard! Ethics and Pollution of the Environment
(SRT/Church of Scotland Video 1984)

A 30-minute video exploring the problems of nuclear waste disposal, lead in petrol and 'acid rain'. It argues for informed judgement and responsible attitude to the environment for the good of our own and future generations. Available for hire direct from the Church of

Scotland Audio-Visual Centre, 121 George Street, Edinburgh. Charge £2.50 (VAT incl).

Make the Most of It (£1.50)
(SRT 1980)

Offers detailed guidelines on energy conservation in church buildings, extracted from the practical experience and knowledge gained through the Church Energy Conservation Scheme.

Fair Shares? An Ethical Guide to Tax and Social Security (£2.50)
by Tony Walter
(SRT/Handsel Press 1985)

A guide to our present income tax and social security arrangements, a description of some major proposals for reform and suggestions for how we can evaluate them.

Will the Future Work? (£3.75)
Howard Davis and David Gosling (editors)
(SRT/WCC Church and Society, 1986)

Focussing on declining industrial areas as well as new industries like micro-electronics, this book explores ways in which church, regional and international bodies can make an informed and practical response in a time of rapid change.

Discussion Papers (£1.50 each)

Occasional series of collected papers on topics of current concern. Each folder is designed to promote informed discussion. Suitable for individual reading or as a basis for group discussion. – Computing and social responsibility (1985).

Ethics and Defence – Power and Responsibility in the Nuclear Age
Howard Davis (editor)
(SRT/Basil Blackwell due 1986)

An integrated collection of essays by an ecumenical and multi-disciplinary study group. Many familiar themes in the defence debate are shown in a new light and the book is an important step forward in a theological and ethical understanding of the subject.

Books and a full list of publications resources are available from:

> The Director
> SRT Project
> Church of Scotland Offices
> 121 George Street
> Edinburgh EH2 4YN.